A Table for Two

SHARON O'CONNOR'S MENUS AND MUSIC

A TABLE FOR TWO

BY
SHARON O'CONNOR

RECIPES FROM CELEBRATED CITY RESTAURANTS
ROMANTIC JAZZ BALLADS BY THE KENNY BARRON ENSEMBLE

MENUS AND MUSIC PRODUCTIONS, INC.
EMERYVILLE, CALIFORNIA

Food photographs copyright © 2004 by Paul Moore
Music instrument photographs copyright © 2004 by Kirk Crippens

Daniel Boulud's recipes on pages 72–76 are from Café Boulud Cookbook, French-American Recipes for the Home Cook by Daniel Boulud and Dorie Greenspan (published by Scribner, New York, 1999)

Every effort has been made to locate the copyright holders of materials used in this book. Should there be any omissions or errors, we apologize and shall be pleased to make the appropriate acknowledgments in future editions.

Printed in Korea

Library of Congress Catalog Card Number: 2004110256
O'Connor, Sharon
Menus and Music Volume XIX
A Table for Two
    Recipes from Celebrated City Restaurants
    Romantic Jazz Ballads by the Kenny Barron Ensemble

Includes Index
1. Cookery 2. Entertaining
I. Title

ISBN 1-883914-36-1 (paperback with music compact disc)

Menus and Music Productions, Inc.
1462 66th Street
Emeryville, CA 94608
(510) 658-9100
www.menusandmusic.com

Book and cover design: Jennifer Barry Design, Fairfax, California
Layout production: Kristen Wurz
Food photographer: Paul Moore
Food stylist: Amy Nathan
Prop stylist: Sara Slavin

10 9 8 7 6 5 4

Titles in the Menus and Music Series

～

Holidays

Dinners for Two

Nutcracker Sweet

Music and Food of Spain

Picnics

Dining and the Opera in Manhattan

Lighthearted Gourmet

Rock & Roll Diner

The Irish Isle

Afternoon Tea Serenade

Spa

Bistro

Italian Intermezzo

Tasting the Wine Country

Museum Cafés & Arts

Dining at Great American Lodges

A Table for Two

～

Contents

INTRODUCTION

I could never have finished this book without jazz! I tested the recipes while listening to the CD that accompanies this book and fell in love with the music all over again during many dinners for two. Although I find the CD to be so listenable that it's hardly left my disc player since it was recorded, of course there were other jazz recordings and KCSM, my local jazz radio station, to keep me going.

What an honor it was to work with these remarkably talented chefs and prodigiously gifted musicians. The past year has been filled with lots of cooking, meeting chefs at great restaurants across America, eating way too much food, and recording the Kenny Barron Ensemble. I wouldn't have missed any of it for the world!

The recipes in this book offer a contemporary approach to good eating, and I know they're dishes you'll want to try. I asked chefs at some of the most romantic restaurants in America to contribute recipes for a dinner for two and adapted their recipes so that you can make them at home. The restaurants are in cities that have long been jazz epicenters, and the menus are perfect for occasions when you want to enjoy a special, leisurely dining experience. Included are recipes by chefs whose cross-cultural cooking is vibrating with excitement, dishes for vegetarians, and creative interpretations of traditional French, Italian, Asian, and American cuisine. I hope you'll set aside time for making dinner a sensational experience. Cooking like this is a way for us all to enjoy life, to live it up while creating our own table for two.

You can re-create an entire menu, or make just one new recipe and fill in with dishes already in your repertoire. If you're planning a dinner party for four or six, increase the amounts in the recipes correspondingly, and whenever possible, use local organic ingredients that are in season.

I hope the recipes inspire you to do some improvising of your own in the kitchen. Some of the best dishes I've ever made happened when I adapted a recipe to emphasize the tastiest ingredient I brought home from the market that day, or when I didn't have an ingredient and substituted another. Include extra tomatoes, use less sugar, add a little more vanilla—this is the kind of improvising that makes cooking fun, especially when you're listening to Kenny Barron, Bob Sheppard, Dave Ellis, Peter Barshay, and Lewis Nash improvise!

When selecting the tunes for this recording project, I chose some of my favorite ballads and jazz standards. Although I was trained as a classical musician and played the piano, harpsichord, and cello as a music major at college, jazz has always had my appreciative ear. My Dad was a band leader, arranger, and singer who played the trumpet and saxophone professionally during the 1940s and '50s. While I was growing up, our family was always listening to music: an eclectic assortment of chamber music, symphonies, musicals, and jazz.

My friend Peter Barshay, a brilliant bass player who definitely appreciates fine food, arranged the tunes with this extraordinary group of musicians in mind. His arrangements provided a structure and an approach that left lots of room for personal expression so that each player's style could come together in the mix. This stellar quintet played with immense musicality, and their performances are both timeless and timely. Working with them in the recording studio was complete joy!

Jazz is performed by musicians whose ears and intuitions tell them what to do. Their music catches the rhythm of our American cities, and places that celebrate jazz tend to celebrate fine cooking as well. Every musician I've had the pleasure of getting to know appreciates fine cooking, and of course great chefs orchestrate their menus. Chefs and jazz musicians are constantly incorporating change into their menus and their music. By reinterpreting traditional dishes and fusing flavors from many of the world's great cuisines, chefs keep their food fresh and exciting, and jazz musicians are playing with the rhythm and harmonies of every culture in gorgeously unexpected ways.

Dinnertime is a perfect opportunity for making great music part of everyday life, and it can create a mood that sustains a world of relaxation and romance. When we enjoy fine food and great music together, we increase the chance of experiencing moments that enrich life, elevate our spirits, and provide the balance we need in a hectic world.

Since food, music and art are three of my inseparable passions, I am excited to present some of Henri Matisse's *Jazz* paper-cuts. After all, Matisse felt that he was creating visual jazz when he created his stunning images.

A Table for Two presents dishes that draw from many cultures, styles, and eras. The dishes are richly diverse and distinctly American, just like the gorgeous jazz recorded here. I hope the music makes you want to dance in the kitchen or at least after dinner! Here's to great music, delicious dinners, and many magical evenings!

—SHARON O'CONNOR

Music Notes

The inspiration for this recording project was *Ballads*, the supremely beautiful John Coltrane Quartet album. But one of many albums created by the legendary quartet of John Coltrane, McCoy Tyner, Jimmy Garrison, and Elvin Jones, *Ballads* is a classic in the best sense of the word, meaning that it is timeless and stands as art. Style and stylists come and go, but this album will simply go on forever. I've been listening to it for more than thirty years and still hear it as the sound of beauty and love. On the CD recorded here, Kenny Barron, Bob Sheppard, Dave Ellis, Peter Barshay, and Lewis Nash pay tribute to these jazz greats by making this selection of ballads their own, keeping them surprising and making them new again.

The recording starts off with "Say it Over and Over Again," the same Jimmy McHugh tune that begins *Ballads*. Although Bob Sheppard doesn't attempt to mimic Coltrane's phrasing and the rest of the group plays in their own unique style, still it's an homage.

John Coltrane's version of "My Favorite Things" by Richard Rodgers was the inspiration for Peter Barshay's arrangement of "Berceuse" by the French composer Gabriel Fauré. Barshay started his career as a classical cellist, and he and I sat in the same cello section of the orchestra at the University of California, Berkeley. It's entirely by coincidence that we worked together on this album so many years later. Kenny Barron and Lewis Nash perform in the Classical Jazz Quartet, a group that adapts classical pieces to jazz settings, so it seemed entirely natural to adapt a classical piece for this project. Jazz has always taken different musical languages and kept them spontaneous while translating them into a swing feeling. Sheppard's solo on "Berceuse" is a dazzling flight of fancy that kicks the piece into high gear.

"Estate"—how quiet and how seductive. Written in 1960 by the Italian singer composer Bruno Martino, "Estate" (summer in Italian) became a commercial success with an interpretation by the Brazilian singer João Gilberto. One of the few Italian compositions that have entered the jazz canon, it is a stunningly beautiful standard that is usually played as a bossa nova.

"The Very Thought of You" is a performance of breathtaking artistry, alive to every nuance, led by Kenny Barron who is one of the finest jazz pianists ever. Barron, Barshay, and Nash played the tune as an instantaneous on-the-spot arrangement. A wonderful, rare experience: there was no need to do a second take—all it would have been was different.

"In a Sentimental Mood" is one of my favorite Duke Ellington tunes. Possibly America's greatest composer, Ellington was also an amazing pianist, a conductor, and a prolific arranger. The world will be forever indebted to him for, in William Blake's phrase, "catching joy as it flies."

On "Blame It On My Youth" by composer Oscar Levant, Kenny Barron, Peter Barshay, and Lewis Nash sustain a gorgeous lyricism and play it like an easy conversation with a friend, all boundaries gone. It was an honor to be present in the studio and hear moments of exchange that only hyper-talented musicians with years of experience can engage in.

"I Only Have Eyes for You" was composed by Harry Warren for the 1934 film *Dames* and was popular during the 1950s thanks to a version by the Flamingos. Barshay's infectiously rhythmic arrangement updates the tune, giving it a new sound.

Kenny Barron's composition "Phantoms" is full of shimmering sorcery, and his solo is masterful, its beauty quite dizzy.

"Very Early" is a tune by the great pianist Bill Evans, who led a groundbreaking trio with drummer Paul Motian and bassist Scott LaFaro. Evans also worked with Miles Davis, who shared his love of the French Impressionist composers Ravel and Debussy. The Miles Davis Quintet masterpiece album *Kind of Blue* featured "Blue in Green," a Bill Evans–Miles Davis ballad. I've always loved "Very Early," and for that matter all of Bill Evans's compositions.

"Alfie" is the title song of the 1966 movie *Alfie*. A well-deserved hit composed by Burt Bacharach, the song originally received a beautiful treatment by saxophonist Sonny Rollins. The performance recorded here is especially poignant.

The quintet really enjoyed improvising on the great blues standard "Stolen Moments" by the renowned arranger, composer, and saxophonist Oliver Nelson.

This album was recorded at Fantasy Studios in Berkeley, and the sessions were a meeting of ears, an opening of hearts, and a chance for us to get together later over one of my home-cooked dinners. These were a few days that I'll remember forever. A mix of East and West Coast players, the sessions brought together New Yorkers

Kenny Barron and Lewis Nash; Peter Barshay and Dave Ellis from the San Francisco Bay Area; and Bob Sheppard from Los Angeles.

Kenny Barron's ability to mesmerize audiences inspired the *Los Angeles Times* to name him one of the top jazz pianists in the world. In the past, he has played with Dizzy Gillespie and Stan Getz, and today he is held in the highest regard by his peers. Barron performs like someone who has lived a full, authentic life, and his elegant, lyrical playing lent style and grace to everything he recorded for this album.

Lewis Nash is one of the most in-demand drummers in the world, and it doesn't take long to figure out why. With feather light brushes, precise sticks, and rumbling cymbal crashes, he built grooves and shifted gaits and patterns. His agile, dynamic playing added layers of rhythm, and it was the binding glue that held the sessions together.

Peter Barshay is a spirited, constantly inventive bass player who has performed with Tony Williams, Freddie Hubbard, and Bobby McFerrin. His exceptional playing on this recording was both solid and sensitive, and his brilliant arrangements gave each tune a structure and an approach from which things could evolve.

Bob Sheppard wove intricate lines on saxophone, flute, and bass clarinet with the elegance and self-assurance of a master, one who has played with everyone from Chick Corea and Steely Dan to Natalie Cole.

Dave Ellis added his big warm sound to the quintet on tenor and soprano saxophone. A rising star, he has been at home performing with the Grateful Dead and leading his own group at the Monterey Jazz Festival.

Whether you're a jazz aficionado or this is one of your first jazz recordings, I know this music will work its magic to create good times. Hopefully, it will also whet your appetite for more jazz and encourage you to step out and support music performed by local musicians and visiting performers.

I've listened to this recording over and over again, and every time I hear something new. The music always transports me out of my everyday world to a better one. You'll just have to listen for yourself!

NOW YOU'RE COOKIN'

At just the right musical moment, the bass player leans over to the piano player and says, "Now you're cookin'." There is nothing accidental in the analogy. I once knew a drummer who, when a tune was going just right, would cry out, "Fry me, Cookie, with a can of lard!" Not the best nutritional advice, perhaps, but once again, the metaphor fits.

Jazz music contains a gustatory rightness, a cuisine counterpart. I've heard chord combinations as fortunate as recipes: savory, succulent, full of variety and surprise—no matter how often they get used. When "Blame It on My Youth" moves from Gmin7 to F#7b5 to Fmin7 to Edim7 (on the words "when first we kissed"), the result is as delicious as the combination of mushrooms, veal stock, finely diced shallot, butter, court bouillon and heavy cream in Morel Sauce.

Sitting down before a keyboard to play "The Very Thought of You" is like standing before a cutting board in a generous kitchen. Fingers move across the keys with all the joy of mincing: the percussive parting of global onions with a large Chinese knife, tenderly trimming Belgian endive, or removing the blouse from a clove of garlic. The work may be mindless (you've done it a thousand times) but it has to be done right. Choosing the right key is like preparing a cheese platter. I have my favorites: playing in the key of Gruyere or Feta or Stilton or Brie.

Playing jazz resembles what takes place in a large pot boiling with improvisation, ingredients sautéed in a pan (scallops converted to golden brown from chalk white), or a match up of materials simmering with delicate fretfulness. By the time you reach the stage of ingestion (and the miracle of metabolism), the ingredients have been appropriately moved—as all things are—by love. As in the song "Say It Over and Over Again," those three words whispered in stories and plays ("I love you") are transformed into something truly magical—whether it be an extraordinary meal or a musical phrase.

—BILL MINOR

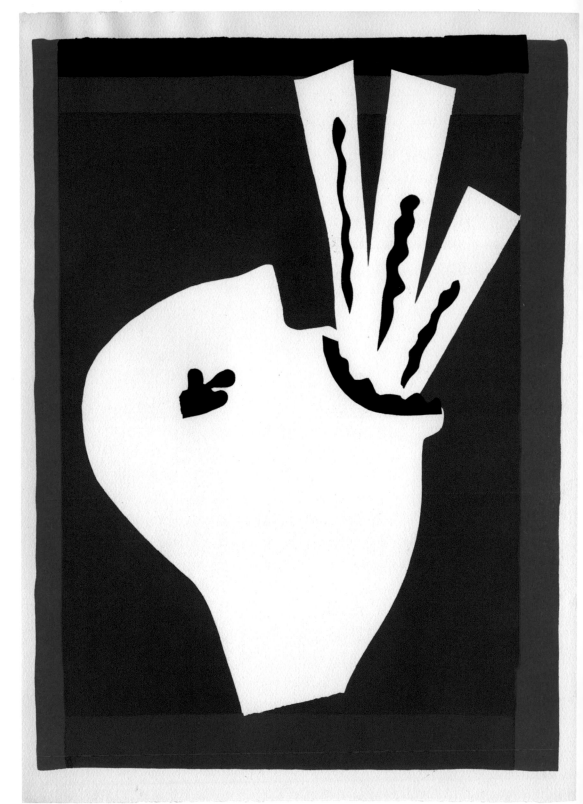

Happy are those who sing
with all their heart,
with the integrity of their heart.
To find Joy in the sky,
in the trees, in the flowers.
There are flowers everywhere
for those who want to see them.

—Henri Matisse

Taj Mahal's Deep-Fried Turkey Recipe for Horace Silver

The following is a transcription of a story told by singer/guitarist Taj Mahal to bassist Peter Barshay. Taj recalls learning a Cajun deep-fried turkey recipe and serving the dish at a party after the Grammys to Horace Silver, the great jazz pianist and composer.

This is a story about when we won the first Grammy. The Phantom Blues Band was an organization I put together in the early 90s. We did a series of albums that started with *Dancing the Blues* and then *Phantom Blues*. At the time of Phantom Blues, we dubbed that group of musicians the Phantom Blues Band. Then we did *Señor Blues*, which was called *Señor Blues* because it was one of my favorite Horace Silver songs. The history of that song with me is that in transferring out to California, I came through Detroit with a friend of mine, a guitar player, and the two of us played in Detroit. I remember listening to "Song for My Father" by Horace. I heard it in a particular light in Detroit in the afternoon when the day was going down and slipping into the night. I was laying down in the afternoon and that song came up on the radio—I always had the radio on wherever I went. I heard "Song for My Father."

Of course when I came out to California, one thing that was different was that you had R & B stations that were on 24 hours, so I was really excited about that. I was in Los Angeles first, and then I came up to the Bay Area. There was a soul food restaurant up on Divisadero Street. I can't remember the name of it. I remember that when I was at the Bill Graham office down on Market Street, I used to walk all the way down Divisadero to this restaurant. One of the things that was great about the restaurant was that they had a jukebox, and the juke had "Señor Blues," "Song for My Father," and lots of blues. My favorite thing was to go in around 2 o'clock, after the lunch crowd had gone through. After everything had quieted down, I would come in and put my money in the jukebox and play "Señor Blues."

That's a little bit of background on Horace and "Señor Blues." The coming together of this whole thing is that one of the things that I like to do is, I like to cook. I'm always looking for interesting ways to cook things.

Anyway, I had go to a blues concert in Vermont or New Hampshire. As we pulled up, I saw these huge metal garbage cans set on top of these gas burners, and I'm wondering what's going on. We got out, and somebody said: "Hey man, you oughta taste these here turkeys. Man they'll taste real good, and they're gonna be coming outta here in just about 5 minutes. Man, we all just got up here from New Orleans. We're a bunch of Cajuns, and we've got these deep-fried turkeys." They marinated the turkeys, infused the meat with this sauce, and cooked them in all this hot oil. And anyway and anyhow, it was really good. So I promised myself that one day I'm gonna learn how to do this.

So the *Señor Blues* album came out, and we found that we were nominated for a Grammy. So there was a big party that happened before the Grammys, and we went to the party. I was absolutely shocked to see Horace there. Nobody knew he was out there, that he knew anything about it. We were coming up on my birthday, which one I don't remember, it was a 50 something anyway. I got in touch with Horace and told him we were going to have sort of an after party. We decided it would be a really nice thing to combine a birthday party and a personal celebration of winning the Grammy. We made the party a not-quite-potluck, but everybody brought a dish. So I prepared the turkeys. I think one was 19 pounds, and the other one was 22 pounds. I bought them at a very good Kosher market. I figured there was going to be a number of people there, and once they taste this thing, it was gonna be over. I made up a garlic marinade, and then to that I added a little bit of Jamaican spices. I let the marinade sit for a long time so that everything infused. I put in a little bit of hot sauce, a Caribbean hot sauce or a pepper sauce, a bit of cumin, some turmeric, a little pickapepper sauce . . . let me think of what else . . . and just a tiny bit of olive oil. I don't use very much salt; if I used any salt at all, I used this Cajun seasoning. I let it sit overnight in the refrigerator. I used a jerk rub that infused the outside of the turkey. I used 5 gallons of peanut oil, and I used a 40 to 60 quart soup pot. It had a retainer at the bottom so the turkey didn't touch the bottom. You have your gas bottle and you have your flame that's up under there. Then you heat this up, and you have a thermometer and you heat it up to 375°F. I put the turkeys in, and the 18 pounder was cooked in about 55 minutes. When you cook it like this it seals the outside, and the turkey cooks in its own juices and everything from the skin down to the bone is absolutely delicious. This makes the meat absolutely succulent down to the bone.

We took the first turkey out, set it aside, and it drained. We started cutting on it, and it took all of about 30 minutes for that turkey to be gone. Horace definitely had a piece of the turkey. The first one went so fast, maybe it was more like 20 minutes before it was gone. Soon! So I cooked the second one. All that was left was a carcass, and everyone kept talking about oh wow man, this turkey, oh wow.

That was just that one particular time, and it was really nice. Hardly anybody left until it finally got to be about 9 or 10 o'clock, and then people started going away. So many people from different parts of the music business came together to hang out with one another. It was a very nice day. We all felt very good that we had the chance to do this since Horace didn't get the Grammy, but it was definitely his song that got the Grammy. And the food was definitely part of it. It was a very nice thing. I really felt good about doing that. Needless to say, the turkey was the hit of the party along with everyone else's food. No food was leftover. They were all really good cooks.

A WARM SUMMER IN SAN FRANCISCO

Although I watched and waited for it every day,
somehow I missed it, the moment when everything reached
the peak of ripeness. It wasn't at the solstice; that was only
the time of the longest light. It was sometime after that, when
the plants had absorbed all that sun, had taken it into themselves
for food and swelled to the height of fullness. It was in July,
in a dizzy blaze of heat and fog, when on some nights
it was too hot to sleep, and the restaurants set half their tables
on the sidewalks; outside the city, down the coast,
the Milky Way floated overhead, and shooting stars
fell from the sky over the ocean. One day the garden
was almost overwhelmed with fruition:

My sweet peas struggled out of the raised bed onto the mulch
of laurel leaves and bark and pods, their brilliantly colored
sunbonnets of rose and streaked pink, magenta and deep purple
pouring out a perfume that was almost oriental. Black-eyed Susans
stared from the flower borders, the orange cherry tomatoes
were sweet as candy, the corn fattened in its swaths of silk,
hummingbirds spiraled by in pairs, the bees gave up
and decided to live in the lavender. At the market,
surrounded by black plums and rosy plums and sugar prunes
and white-fleshed peaches and nectarines, perfumey melons
and mangoes, purple figs in green plastic baskets,
clusters of tiny Champagne grapes and piles of red-black cherries
and apricots freckled and streaked with rose, I felt tears
come into my eyes, absurdly, because I knew
that summer had peaked and was already passing
away. I felt very close then to understanding
the mystery: It seemed to me that I almost knew
what it meant to be alive, as if my life had swelled
to some high moment of response, as if I could
reach out and touch the season, as if I were inside
its body, surrounded by sweet pulp and juice,
shimmering veins and ripened skin.

—CAROLYN MILLER

AVALON
Toronto, Ontario

For Avalon chef Chris McDonald, a fine dinner is composed like a piece of music, with the courses working together to create a culinary experience that has an orchestrated beginning, middle, and end.

Avalon is located in the heart of Toronto's theater district, just blocks from Roy Thomson Hall, which is home to the Toronto Symphony Orchestra. The restaurant's serene, understated dining room has large windows, cream-colored walls, and crisp white tablecloths that provide an elegant background for special occasions and chef McDonald's masterful cooking.

Before opening Avalon, McDonald studied and cooked in France, Italy, New York, Mexico, the San Francisco Bay Area, and New Mexico. His contemporary cuisine combines traditional techniques with ingredients and flavors from around the world. Chef McDonald changes his menu daily and hopes that his cooking will transport diners to new places and cultures.

Along with a traditional à la carte menu, the restaurant offers a six-course gastronomic menu and a special Friday-night Adventure Menu. Every Friday, guests are invited to join McDonald on a ten- to twelve-course voyage featuring small dishes that use exceptional ingredients and a single cooking technique, such as raw, seared, or braised. The courses are unannounced, so diners are surprised by each plate. Every dish is paired with a beverage, which may include wine, beer, sake, or a specialty cocktail created in the kitchen rather than at the bar. Avalon's food-friendly wine list has received *Wine Spectator* magazine's Award of Excellence. Along with daily menu meetings, the loyal restaurant staff receives frequent wine tutoring and can help diners create interesting and successful food and wine pairings. They are committed to enhancing each guest's experience, and excellent service is a restaurant hallmark.

A meal at Avalon is like a brilliant performance where timing, technique, flavor, and atmosphere create an exceptional experience that lingers long after the last plate has been cleared. The following recipes were created by chef Chris McDonald and presented to Menus and Music.

Menu

Halibut Steamed with Shiso and Radishes

~

Roast Beef Tenderloin with Winter Vegetables
and Veronese Pepper and Bread Sauce

~

Olive Oil Cake with
Fennel Pollen–Honey Mousse
and Toasted Almonds

Halibut Steamed with Shiso and Radishes

An elegant dish that perfectly balances fresh, delicate flavors.

Two Pacific halibut or John Dory fillets
  (3 ounces each), skinned
Tangerine Salt (recipe follows)
White pepper to taste
2 fresh shiso leaves*
8 ounces Easter egg radishes* or red
  radishes, trimmed

½ cup chicken stock (see Basics) or
  canned low-salt chicken broth
½ cup water
1 small shallot, minced
Salt to taste
2 teaspoons salted butter

✦ Sprinkle each fish fillet with tangerine salt and white pepper. Top each fillet with a shiso leaf. Place the fish on a plate that will fit into your steamer; do not overlap the pieces. Cover the plate tightly with plastic wrap.

✦ Slice the radishes into thin coins. In a small frying pan, bring the stock or broth, water, and shallot to a boil over medium-high heat. Add the radishes and a pinch of salt and white pepper. Cook until half the liquid evaporates. Add the butter, shaking the pan to coat the radishes, and cook until glazed. Sprinkle with a little more salt. Remove from the heat and set aside.

✦ Place the plate with the fish in a steamer basket. Place in the steamer over boiling water. Cover and steam for 4 to 7 minutes, or until the fish is opaque throughout. Arrange the radishes in the center of each of 2 warmed plates and top them with a shiso leaf–topped fish fillet; serve at once. *Makes 2 servings*

*Available at specialty produce stores and some supermarkets (see Glossary).

(continued)

TANGERINE SALT

¼ cup kosher salt   2 small pieces dried tangerine peel*

✦ In a spice grinder or food processor, combine the salt and tangerine peel and process until powdered. Store in an airtight container. *Makes ¼ cup*

*Dried tangerine peel may be purchased in Asian markets, or you can cut strips of tangerine zest (see Basics) and dry them in a low oven.

The saxophone is actually a translation of the human voice, in my conception. All you can do is play melody. No matter how complicated it gets, it's still a melody.

—STAN GETZ

Roast Beef Tenderloin with Winter Vegetables and Veronese Pepper and Bread Sauce

Rare slices of beef tenderloin and boiled vegetables are served with a traditional peppery Italian sauce.

12 ounces beef tenderloin

Olive oil for coating

Salt and freshly ground pepper to taste

2 cups beef stock (see Basics) or
   canned low-salt beef broth

2 carrots, peeled and chopped

2 parsnips, peeled and chopped

6 small Brussels sprouts

2 small Yukon Gold potatoes, peeled
   and quartered

1½ cups canned beef consommé,
   heated

Veronese Pepper and Bread Sauce
   (recipe follows)

✦ Preheat the oven to 450°F. Coat the beef tenderloin with olive oil, and sprinkle with salt and pepper.

✦ In a large ovenproof sauté pan, sear the tenderloin on all sides over high heat. Transfer the pan to the preheated oven and roast the tenderloin for 10 minutes. Remove from the oven and set aside.

✦ Meanwhile, pour the stock or broth into a large pot and bring to a simmer over medium heat. Add the carrots and cook until tender. Repeat with each kind of vegetable.

✦ Divide the vegetables between 2 large warmed soup plates. Cut the beef into ½-inch-thick slices and arrange 2 or 3 slices on top of the vegetables. Ladle the heated consommé into each bowl and serve. Pass the sauce at the table.

Makes 2 servings

Veronese Pepper and Bread Sauce

This spicy sauce is traditionally served with bollito misto, *a boiled dinner of meats and vegetables that is common in northern Italy.*

¼ cup unsalted butter at room
  temperature
2 ounces beef or veal bone marrow,*
  soaked in cold water in the
  refrigerator overnight

½ cup dried bread crumbs
1¼ cups beef stock (see Basics) or
  canned low-salt beef broth
Salt to taste
¾ tablespoon freshly ground pepper

✦ In a food processor, combine the butter and marrow and process until blended. Transfer the marrow mixture to a heavy saucepan. Cook over low heat until the mixture melts. Strain through a fine-mesh sieve into a bowl. Return to the saucepan over low heat and stir in the bread crumbs. Cook for 15 minutes, stirring occasionally. Stir in the broth or stock, salt, and pepper and cook for 30 minutes over low heat, stirring occasionally. Use now, or store tightly covered, in the refrigerator for up to 1 week. Serve warm. *Makes about 2 cups*

*Bone marrow is available at butcher shops and in some supermarkets.

Olive Oil Cake with Fennel Pollen–Honey Mousse and Toasted Almonds

A luscious rolled cake filled with anise-flavored mousse and topped with whipped cream and toasted almonds. The olive oil cake is also delicious served plain.

2 eggs, separated

1 egg white (save the extra yolk for the mousse)

¼ cup sugar

1 teaspoon grated lemon zest or orange zest

⅓ cup all-purpose flour

Pinch of salt

2 tablespoons sherry

3 tablespoons extra-virgin olive oil

Fennel Pollen–Honey Mousse (recipe follows)

⅓ cup heavy cream, stiffly whipped

1 cup slivered almonds, toasted (see Basics)

✦ Preheat the oven to 375°F. Butter and flour an 8-inch square baking dish and line it with parchment paper.

✦ In a large bowl, using an electric mixer, beat the 2 egg yolks with the sugar until pale and a ribbon forms on the surface when the beaters are lifted. Stir in the zest.

✦ In a small bowl, combine the flour and salt. Stir well. Add the flour mixture to the egg mixture and stir until blended. Stir in the sherry and olive oil.

✦ In a large bowl, beat the 3 egg whites until stiff, glossy peaks form. Fold the egg whites into the batter.

✦ Pour the batter into the prepared pan and bake for 15 minutes, or until a skewer inserted into the center comes out clean. Let the cake cool for at least 20 minutes.

✦ To assemble: Evenly spread the mousse over the cake. Holding the parchment paper down beneath the cake at one short end of the pan, carefully roll the cake into a jelly roll.

✦ Cover the outside of the roll with whipped cream and sprinkle it with the toasted almonds. Slice crosswise into 1-inch-thick pieces. Arrange a slice on each of 2 plates, and serve at once. *Makes 1 cake*

FENNEL POLLEN–HONEY MOUSSE

2 tablespoons honey

2 egg yolks

Pinch of salt

½ cup whole milk

2 teaspoons fennel pollen,* or

   1 teaspoon anise extract

1 teaspoon unflavored gelatin powder

2 tablespoons water

⅓ cup heavy cream

✦ In a medium bowl, using an electric mixer on high speed, beat the honey, egg yolks, and salt together until pale.

✦ In a small saucepan, combine the milk and fennel pollen or anise extract. Cook over medium heat until bubbles form around the edges of the pan. Remove the pan from heat, cover with plastic wrap, and let stand for 10 minutes.

✦ In a cup, sprinkle the gelatin over the water. Let soak. Whisk a little of the milk mixture into the egg mixture. Stir in the rest of the milk mixture and strain through a fine-mesh sieve into the saucepan. Cook over medium heat, stirring constantly, until the custard coats the back of a spoon; do not let boil. Remove from heat and stir in the gelatin mixture. Let cool. Refrigerate for at least 2 hours.

✦ In a deep bowl, beat the cream until soft peaks form. Fold the whipped cream into the chilled custard. *Makes 1 cup*

*Fennel pollen is available at some specialty foods stores (see Glossary and Resources).

BACCHANALIA

Atlanta, Georgia

Since 1993, Bacchanalia has served flawless contemporary American cuisine to legions of fans in Atlanta. With a relaxed elegant setting and an imaginative seasonal menu based on locally grown organic produce and carefully selected meats and seafood, Bacchanalia is regularly named Atlanta's finest restaurant.

Co-owners and chefs Anne Quatrano and Clifford Harrison have been cooking together since they met as students at the California Culinary Academy in San Francisco. After working as a team at Bimini Twist, La Petite Ferme, and the Grolier Club in New York, the couple decided to move back to Summerland Farm, Quatrano's family property in Cartersville, Georgia. Much of the organic produce used in Bacchanalia's kitchen is grown at Summerland Farm, which is also home to many horses, Jersey cows, pigs, goats, hens, and an assortment of domestic animals.

In January 2000, Bacchanalia moved from its original location to a revamped industrial space on the Westside of midtown Atlanta. The glazed-ceramic-tile walls and tall steel windows with views of the midtown skyline are softened by the chocolate mohair banquettes and beige window shades. A private dining area is enclosed by airy floor-to-ceiling curtains. The bustling kitchen is set behind glass walls, and diners can choose to sit at the bar and watch Bacchanalia chefs in action. As guests enter the restaurant, they pass through Star Provisions, Quatrano and Harrison's gourmet products store. Here, Atlanta residents can purchase artisanal cheeses, seafood, meats, stylish tableware, and freshly baked goods from the Bacchanalia ovens.

Bacchanalia's fixed-price four-course menu has multiple options for each course and features intricately prepared dishes that balance flavors and textures to create subtle complexities. An extensive wine list chosen by chef Harrison complements the cuisine, and the friendly, knowledgeable staff is available to suggest wine and food pairings. Bacchanalia consistently receives top Zagat ratings, and the restaurant is a Mobil four-star award winner. The following recipes were created by chefs Anne Quatrano and Clifford Harrison and presented to Menus and Music.

Menu

Prosciutto with Fresh Fig Preserves

~

Melon Sorbet with French Feta Cheese

~

Roasted Halibut with Braised Baby Tomatoes

~

Lemon Buttermilk Panna Cotta
with Macerated Blackberries

Prosciutto with Fresh Fig Preserves

Tender, delicately flavored prosciutto and ripe figs with hints of ginger and lemon pair beautifully in this appetizer.

1 pound figs, stemmed and halved, plus
   4 figs for garnish
2 cups sugar
Juice of ½ lemon

¼ teaspoon grated fresh ginger
4 slices prosciutto
½ teaspoon aged balsamic vinegar

✦ In a medium nonreactive saucepan, combine the halved figs and the sugar. Cover and let stand at room temperature for 24 hours.

✦ Add the lemon juice and ginger and place the saucepan over low heat. Cook, stirring occasionally, for 45 minutes, or until the liquid runs clear and the figs are soft. Remove from heat and transfer the figs to a bowl to cool.

✦ To serve, arrange 2 prosciutto slices on each of 2 plates and top with the fig preserves. Garnish each plate with 4 fig halves and dots of balsamic vinegar.

Makes 2 servings

Jazz will endure just as long as people hear it through their feet instead of their brains. —John Philip Sousa

Melon Sorbet with French Feta Cheese

A sublime combination of flavors. The light and refreshing sorbet is especially delicious made with ambrosia melon, which has pale orange flesh and a flowery, very sweet flavor.

SORBET

1 ambrosia melon or cantaloupe,
  seeded and peeled

½ tablespoon fresh lemon juice

¼ cup simple syrup (see Basics)

Pinch of salt

4 ounces (½ cup) French sheep's milk
  feta cheese

½ tablespoon honey

Fresh mint sprigs (optional)

✦ Cut the melon into 4 quarters. Cover 1 piece with plastic wrap and reserve it in the refrigerator. Peel and coarsely chop the remaining melon.

✦ In a food processor or blender, purée the chopped melon, lemon juice, simple syrup, and salt. Strain the purée through a fine-mesh sieve into a bowl. Cover and refrigerate for 2 hours. Freeze in an ice cream machine according to the manufacturer's instructions.

✦ To serve, cut the reserved melon into very thin slices. Cover the bottom of 2 chilled plates with the slices. Crumble or shave the feta cheese over the melon slices. Place a scoop of melon sorbet on the plate and drizzle with honey. If desired, garnish with mint sprigs. *Makes 2 servings*

ROASTED HALIBUT WITH BRAISED BABY TOMATOES

2 tablespoons olive oil, plus more
    for drizzling
½ sweet white or red onion,
    finely diced
2 garlic cloves, thinly sliced
1 pound small tomatoes, peeled
    (see Basics)

½ cup chicken stock or vegetable
    stock (see Basics) or canned low-salt
    chicken broth
Salt and freshly ground pepper to taste
2 fresh basil leaves, plus sprigs
    for garnish
2 Pacific halibut fillets, or other
    mild white fish
½ tablespoon unsalted butter

✦ Preheat the oven to 400°F.

✦ In a saucepan, heat 1 tablespoon of the olive oil over medium heat, and sauté
the onion and garlic for 3 minutes, or until translucent. Add the tomatoes, stock
or broth, salt, pepper, and basil leaves and cook until the tomatoes soften, about
20 minutes. Remove from heat. Set aside and keep warm.

✦ In a large ovenproof sauté pan, heat the remaining 1 tablespoon olive oil over
medium-high heat. Season the halibut fillets with salt and pepper and cook for
about 2 minutes on each side, or until lightly browned. Transfer to the preheated
oven and bake for 5 minutes, or until the fish is opaque throughout.

✦ To serve, stir the butter into the tomatoes until it melts. Spoon the braised
tomatoes into each of 2 deep plates and top with a halibut fillet. Garnish with a
drizzle of olive oil and basil sprigs and serve at once. *Makes 2 servings*

Lemon Buttermilk Panna Cotta
with Macerated Blackberries

A perfectly delicious pairing. The silky, eggless custards can be made a day or two in advance.

½ tablespoon unflavored gelatin

1 cup buttermilk

½ cup heavy cream

¼ cup sugar

½ tablespoon fresh lemon juice

Grated zest of ¼ lemon (see Basics)

¼ inch vanilla bean, split lengthwise,
    or ¼ teaspoon vanilla extract

Macerated Blackberries
    (recipe follows)

✦ In a medium bowl, stir together the gelatin and buttermilk. Set aside.

✦ In a heavy saucepan, combine the cream, sugar, lemon zest, and vanilla bean, if using. Bring to a boil over medium heat. Remove from heat.

✦ Stir the lemon juice into the buttermilk mixture. Add the buttermilk mixture and vanilla extract, if using, to the cream mixture and stir until smooth. Pour the mixture through a fine-mesh sieve into 2 oiled 6-ounce ramekins or molds. Let cool to room temperature. Refrigerate until chilled, at least 4 hours. To serve, unmold a panna cotta in the center of each of 2 plates. Spoon the macerated blackberries over. *Makes 2 servings*

Macerated Blackberries

1 pint fresh blackberries

¼ cup sugar

1 small sprig fresh lavender, slightly
    bruised

Juice of ½ lemon

✦ In a medium bowl, gently stir together all the ingredients. Set aside to macerate for 1 hour at room temperature. *Makes about 2 cups*

THE RESTAURANT AT HOTEL BEL-AIR
Los Angeles, California

From the moment guests cross the arched stone bridge near Hotel
Bel-Air's signature Swan Lake, they enter a storybook land of luxury
and tranquility. The hotel is a twelve-acre oasis in a wooded canyon
near Beverly Hills and only one-half mile from famed Sunset Boulevard.
Intimate courtyards, gurgling fountains, an oval swimming pool, and pink
mission-style bungalows are scattered throughout the luxuriant gardens. Long
a favorite of Hollywood stars, the Bel-Air opened in 1946 and soon became a
favorite hideaway for celebrities such as Grace Kelly, Cary Grant, and Marilyn
Monroe. Today, the guestrooms and suites feature private garden entrances,
fireplaces, country French décor, and guests can even enjoy complimentary
afternoon tea service in the privacy of their own room. This Mobile Five-Star
award-winning hotel offers romance and privacy and a staff whose service
is legendary.

A before-dinner stroll through the gardens reveals soaring trees, lush
tropical foliage, and scented blossoms. One of the most romantic places to
dine in Los Angeles, The Restaurant at Hotel Bel-Air includes a formal dining
room as well as year-round alfresco dining on the arcaded terrace. Draped in
bougainvillea blossoms, The Terrace has heated terra-cotta flooring and
cushioned banquettes that overlook Swan Lake and the gardens.

The Restaurant's California and Mediterranean cuisine showcases the
freshest produce and seafood, specialty meats, and handcrafted cheeses
prepared by executive chef Douglas Dodd. His seasonal menus blend classic
flavors with contemporary cooking techniques. The property's herb garden is
unbelievably large, and a variety of aromatic herbs are picked for the kitchen
daily. Table One, the private chef's table located in the kitchen, is the perfect
setting for a special seven-course lunch or dinner. The Restaurant has one of
southern California's largest collections of fine wine, Champagne, and port,
with more than thirty thousand bottles cellared under the hotel in what was
once a tunnel for horse riders. In The Bar, a cozy fireplace, wood paneling,

and jazz performed nightly on the baby grand create a comfortable, elegant atmosphere for neighborhood regulars and visiting celebrities.

One of the greatest luxuries—a beautiful setting where it's possible to forget all worldly cares—is the hallmark of this celebrated restaurant. Diners enjoy exceptional cuisine in an atmosphere of romance, intimacy, and comfort. The following recipes were created by executive chef Douglas Dodd and presented to Menus and Music.

Menu

Shrimp and Crab Cobb Salad
with Spicy Rémoulade

~

Halibut with Garden Vegetables,
Potato-Herb Galettes, and Spring Pea Sauce

~

Apple and Sun-Dried Cherry Crisp
with Vanilla Bean Ice Cream

SHRIMP AND CRAB COBB SALAD
WITH SPICY RÉMOULADE

A luxurious seafood salad with perfectly balanced tastes, colors, and textures. Serve, with the piquant rémoulade sauce alongside, as a first course or as a main-dish salad with crusty bread.

SPICY RÉMOULADE

½ cup mayonnaise (for homemade see Basics)

½ teaspoon sambal oelek*

1 teaspoon chopped capers

1 tablespoon minced red onion

½ tomato, peeled, seeded, and finely chopped (see Basics)

1 tablespoon chopped fresh chives

1 tablespoon fresh lemon juice

Salt and freshly ground pepper to taste

LEMON VINAIGRETTE

2 tablespoons fresh lemon juice

1 teaspoon Dijon mustard

Salt and freshly ground pepper to taste

½ teaspoon grated lemon zest (see Basics)

½ teaspoon minced garlic

6 tablespoons extra-virgin olive oil

2 handfuls mixed baby salad greens

2 handfuls chopped romaine lettuce

6 cooked prawns or jumbo shrimp, chopped into bite-sized pieces

4 ounces fresh lump crabmeat

4 slices bacon, fried and crumbled

1 avocado, pitted, peeled, and diced

1 tomato, diced

¼ cup crumbled blue cheese

✦ To make the rémoulade: In a small bowl, stir together all the ingredients until blended. Cover and refrigerate to let the flavors blend.

✦ To make the lemon vinaigrette: In a small bowl, combine the lemon juice, mustard, salt, pepper, lemon zest, and garlic. Whisk in the olive oil in a thin, steady stream until the mixture emulsifies.

✦ In a salad bowl, toss the baby greens, lettuce, and ¼ cup of the lemon vinaigrette together. Arrange the shrimp, crab, crumbled bacon, avocado, tomato, and blue cheese in rows on top. Drizzle with some of the remaining lemon vinaigrette and serve with the rémoulade alongside. *Makes 2 servings*

*Available at Asian markets and specialty foods stores (see Glossary and Resources).

Halibut with Garden Vegetables, Potato-Herb Galettes, and Spring Pea Sauce

Golden-brown halibut fillets and colorful vegetables top crisp galettes, with a ring of green pea sauce. Absolutely gorgeous and delicious.

POTATO-HERB GALETTES

2 leeks, white part only, washed and dried

5 tablespoons olive oil or unsalted butter

1 small onion, cut in half and thinly sliced

1 parsnip, peeled

1 potato, peeled

2 tablespoons minced mixed fresh thyme, parsley, and chives

Salt and freshly ground pepper to taste

3 tablespoons olive oil or unsalted butter

1½ cups finely diced mixed vegetables such as zucchini, squash, and green beans

10 currant tomatoes or halved cherry tomatoes

1 cup mushrooms, diced

2 Pacific halibut fillets, or other mild white fish

Spring Pea Sauce (recipe follows)

Fresh parsley sprigs or chives for garnish (optional)

✦ To make the galettes: Cut the leeks in half lengthwise and slice into thin, long strips. In a sauté pan, heat 1 tablespoon of the olive oil or melt 1 tablespoon of the butter over medium heat. Sauté the leek and onion for 3 minutes, or until soft but not browned. Remove from heat and set aside.

✦ Using the large holes of a box grater, shred the parsnip and potato. In a medium bowl, mix the potato, parsnip, leek mixture, herbs, salt, and pepper together.

✦ In a large sauté pan, heat 2 tablespoons of the olive oil or melt 2 tablespoons of the butter over medium-high heat. Add the potato mixture, cover, and cook, shaking the pan occasionally, for about 10 minutes, or until the bottom of the pancake is browned.

✦ Slide the potato pancake onto a platter. Heat the remaining 2 tablespoons olive oil or butter over medium heat. Invert the plate over the pan to return the potato pancake. Cover and cook, shaking the pan occasionally for 10 minutes, or until browned on the second side. Slide the potato cake onto a platter.

✦ In a medium sauté pan, heat 1 tablespoon of the olive oil or melt 1 tablespoon of the butter over medium heat. Sauté all the vegetables for 5 minutes, or until the squash and/or green beans are crisp-tender. Remove from heat and set aside.

✦ In a large sauté pan, heat the remaining 2 tablespoons olive oil or melt the remaining butter over medium-high heat. Season both sides of the fish with salt and pepper. Place the fish in the hot sauté pan, reduce heat to medium-low, and cook on each side for 5 minutes, or until browned and opaque throughout.

✦ To serve, cut the galette into 4 wedges. Place 2 wedges in the center of each of 2 warmed plates. Spoon the vegetables over the galettes and top with a fish fillet. Spoon the pea sauce around each plate and garnish with parsley or chives, if you like. Serve at once. *Makes 2 servings*

SPRING PEA SAUCE

¾ cup fresh or thawed frozen peas
¼ cup cold water
½ garlic clove
½ shallot

1 tablespoon unsalted butter
Salt and freshly ground white pepper
  to taste

✦ In a food processor or blender, combine the peas, water, garlic, and shallot. Purée. Strain the purée through a fine-mesh sieve into a small saucepan. Place over medium-low heat. Add the butter, salt, and pepper and stir until the butter melts. Serve warm. *Makes about 1 cup*

Apple and Sun-Dried Cherry Crisp with Vanilla Bean Ice Cream

Light, crisp phyllo dough wraps cherries and tender pieces of apple. Serve with a scoop of vanilla bean ice cream and drizzle with luscious cherry sauce.

2 Granny Smith or pippin apples, peeled, cored, and chopped into small bite-sized pieces
½ cup apple juice
½ cup water
½ cup port wine
¼ cup sugar
1 cinnamon stick

½ cup dried sweet cherries
¼ cup cornstarch
1 package frozen phyllo dough, thawed in the refrigerator for 24 hours
½ cup (1 stick) unsalted butter, melted
Vanilla Bean Ice Cream (recipe follows)

✦ Preheat the oven to 450°F. Line a baking sheet with parchment paper or a silpat.

✦ In a large sauté pan, combine the apples, ¼ cup of the water, and ¼ cup of the apple juice. Cook over medium-high heat for 10 minutes, or until the apples are tender. Drain the mixture in a fine-mesh sieve over a bowl. Reserve the apples and liquid.

✦ In a medium saucepan, combine the port, the remaining ¼ cup apple juice, the sugar, and cinnamon stick. Bring to a boil over high heat. Add the cherries and reduce heat to low. Simmer for 5 minutes, or until the cherries are plump and tender. Drain the cherries in a fine-mesh sieve over a small bowl. Reserve the cherries and juice.

✦ In a small bowl, stir the cornstarch and the remaining ¼ cup water together to make a thin paste. Transfer the reserved cherry juice to a small saucepan and bring to a boil. Stir in 1 tablespoon of the cornstarch mixture and cook to make a thin sauce. Remove half of the sauce and transfer it to a bowl; set aside. Boil the remaining sauce with the remaining cornstarch mixture to make a thick jelly.

✦ In a medium bowl, stir the apples, cherries, and cherry jelly together until blended. Cover with plastic wrap and refrigerate until cooled.

(continued)

✦ On a work surface, spread out a sheet of phyllo dough and lightly brush it with melted butter. Keep the remaining phyllo covered with a damp cloth. Place a second phyllo sheet over the first and brush with butter. Repeat with a third sheet and brush with butter. Cut the dough to a 8½-by-10½-inch rectangle.

✦ Place ½ cup of the cooled apple-cherry filling in a narrow 5½-inch-long line in the center of the pastry running crosswise. Fold in 1½ inches of the phyllo over the apple mixture on each side. Brush these sides with butter and roll up the phyllo starting at one of the short sides to form a tube. Brush the entire roll with butter, and place seam-side down on the prepared baking sheet.

✦ Bake the crisp in the preheated oven for 18 minutes, or until golden brown. Remove and let cool for 2 minutes. Using a serrated knife, slice the roll on the diagonal into 4 pieces. Stand a diagonal upright on each of 2 plates. Add a scoop of vanilla ice cream and the cherry sauce; serve at once. *Makes 4 servings*

Vanilla Bean Ice Cream

¼ cup heavy cream

¾ cup milk

¼ cup sugar

½ inch vanilla bean, split lengthwise, or ½ teaspoon vanilla extract

4 egg yolks, beaten

✦ In a medium saucepan, combine the cream, milk, sugar, and vanilla bean, if using. Cook over medium heat until boiling. Remove from heat.

✦ In a medium bowl, whisk the egg yolks until pale and thick. Gradually whisk in half of the hot milk mixture. Return the mixture to the saucepan and cook over medium heat for 3 minutes, stirring constantly until thickened; do not boil. Remove from heat and pour through a fine-mesh sieve into a bowl. Stir in the vanilla extract, if using. Cover with plastic wrap and refrigerate for at least 2 hours. Freeze in an ice cream maker according to the manufacturer's instructions. *Makes 1 pint*

I think I had it in the back of my mind that I wanted to sound like a dry martini.

—PAUL DESMOND

BLUE GINGER
Wellesley, Massachusetts

Blue Ginger is both a beloved neighborhood bistro and a nationally celebrated restaurant. Chef Ming Tsai, who is known to millions from his television cooking shows, opened the restaurant with his wife Polly, in 1998. Today, food-lovers from all over the world travel to Wellesley, a Boston suburb, to experience Tsai's groundbreaking East-West cuisine.

The Tsais designed the restaurant themselves, with the assistance of a feng shui master. Cream-colored walls and Vietnamese waterscapes by artist Daottai Phong are set off by recessed lighting, Italian granite floors, and warm cherry woodwork. A forty-foot blue pearl granite counter allows guests to watch Blue Ginger chefs at work in the open kitchen, and a water sculpture adds to the soothing ambiance. Ming Tsai's favorite color shows up in cobalt accents throughout the restaurant, including his signature blue glassware.

Although Tsai spent hours cooking alongside his parents at their Chinese restaurant in Ohio, he majored in engineering at Yale University before deciding to make a career in the kitchen. He studied at the Cordon Bleu cooking school and then worked with master baker Pierre Hermé at Fauchon, the renowned Parisian food emporium. In order to further expand his culinary horizons, Tsai went on to cook at great restaurants in Paris, San Francisco, Santa Fe, and Tokyo. Thanks to his diverse background, the chef's recipes happily mingle Chinese, Southeast Asian, Japanese, French, and American culinary traditions. Exciting cross-cultural dishes, such as Pomegranate-Marinated Squab with Thai Quince Chutney (see page 62), balance flavors and contrast textures, colors, and temperatures. Blue Ginger's wine list is as eclectic as the restaurant's menu, with carefully chosen selections that complement Tsai's flavorful dishes.

Among Tsai's many awards are the 2002 James Beard Best Chef Northeast and Chef of the Year from *Esquire* magazine. Blue Ginger's friendly, festive atmosphere and one-of-a-kind menu make this restaurant perfect for a family celebration or for a romantic dinner for two. The following recipes were created by chef Ming Tsai and presented to Menus and Music.

Menu

Oysters with Lemongrass Mignonette

~

Pomegranate-Marinated Squab
with Thai Quince Chutney

~

Broiled Lobster Tails with
Orange-Chive Butter

~

Bittersweet Chocolate Cakes with
Chocolate Sauce and Cardamom Cream

OYSTERS WITH LEMONGRASS MIGNONETTE

Spoon this mignonette with a twist over raw oysters to make an elegant starter for special occasions.

1 shallot, finely diced
1 teaspoon minced fresh ginger
1 tablespoon minced lemongrass*

¼ cup fresh lime juice
12 fresh oysters, shucked and returned
    to their deep bottom half shells

✦ In a small bowl, stir the shallot, ginger, lemongrass, and lime juice together. Arrange the oysters on a platter of cracked ice. Spoon the mignonette over the oysters and serve at once. *Makes 2 servings*

*Available at Asian markets and specialty foods stores (see Glossary and Resources).

POMEGRANATE-MARINATED SQUAB WITH THAI QUINCE CHUTNEY

Ming Tsai's seared squab, served with a fiery sweet-tart chutney, is a perfect special-occasion dish. Squab should be cooked medium-rare for the best flavor. The chutney is excellent with all kinds of poultry, or as a sandwich condiment.

¼ cup pomegranate molasses*

¾ cup soy sauce

¾ cup dry red wine

1 tablespoon minced garlic

2 tablespoons minced fresh ginger

¼ cup packed brown sugar

2 squabs, partially boned

Salt and freshly ground pepper to taste

2 tablespoons canola oil

2 tablespoons cold unsalted butter, chopped into pieces

Thai Quince Chutney (recipe follows)

✦ In a baking dish just large enough to hold the squabs, combine the pomegranate molasses, soy sauce, wine, garlic, ginger, and brown sugar. Stir to blend. Add the squabs and let stand at room temperature for about 1 hour, turning the squabs occasionally.

✦ Remove the squabs from the marinade and sprinkle them with salt and pepper. Reserve the marinade.

✦ In a large frying pan, heat the canola oil over medium-high heat. Brown the squabs, turning frequently, for 8 minutes for medium rare. Transfer the squabs to a plate and cover loosely with aluminum foil.

✦ Pour the reserved marinade into the frying pan, stirring to scrape up any browned bits from the bottom of the pan. Cook over medium heat for 6 minutes, or until the liquid reduces by half.

✦ Just before serving, whisk the butter pieces into the sauce. Taste and adjust the seasoning. Place a squab on each of 2 plates and spoon some quince chutney nearby. Drizzle the sauce over and serve at once. *Makes 2 servings*

*Available at Middle Eastern markets, some supermarkets, and specialty foods stores (see Glossary and Resources).

THAI QUINCE CHUTNEY

1 tablespoon canola oil
½ large red onion, finely diced
2 Thai chilies*, minced
Salt and freshly ground pepper to taste

1 large quince, peeled, cored, and
  finely chopped
Juice of ½ lime

✦ Heat a large skillet over medium heat. Swirl in the canola oil and heat until the oil shimmers. Sauté the onion and chilies for 8 minutes, or until browned. Season with salt and pepper. Reduce heat to medium-low, add the quince and lime juice, and cook for 20 minutes, stirring occasionally until the quinces are soft. Taste and adjust the seasoning. Let cool. *Makes about 1 cup*

*Available at Asian markets and some supermarkets (see Glossary).

BROILED LOBSTER TAILS WITH ORANGE-CHIVE BUTTER

5 tablespoons unsalted butter

1 teaspoon minced fresh ginger

2 teaspoons grated orange zest
  (see Basics)

¼ cup Grand Marnier or other
  orange liqueur

2 tablespoons chopped fresh chives

Salt and freshly ground pepper to taste

2 large lobster tails

Thin orange slices for garnish
  (optional)

✦ Preheat the broiler. In a small sauté pan, melt 1 tablespoon of the butter over medium-high heat and sauté the ginger and orange zest for 1 minute. Carefully pour in the Grand Marnier. Using a long-handled match and averting your face, light the liquid; shake the pan until the flames go out. Stir in the remaining 4 tablespoons butter until melted. Stir in half of the chives and season with salt and pepper. Remove from the heat and cover to keep warm.

✦ Using a large, sharp knife, split each lobster tail in half lengthwise. Set the lobster tails on a broiler pan, flesh side up, and brush liberally with the orange-chive butter. Place under the preheated broiler and cook for 4 to 5 minutes, or until opaque. Remove from the oven and brush with more orange-chive butter. Serve at once, garnished with optional orange slices and the chives.

Makes 2 servings

BITTERSWEET CHOCOLATE CAKES WITH CHOCOLATE SAUCE AND CARDAMOM CREAM

These individual flourless chocolate cakes taste even better served with rich chocolate sauce and cardamom-flavored cream.

3 tablespoons water

¼ cup plus ¾ tablespoon sugar

1½ ounces bittersweet chocolate, finely chopped

1¾ ounces unsweetened chocolate, finely chopped

4½ tablespoons cold unsalted butter, cubed

1 extra-large egg at room temperature

CHOCOLATE SAUCE

1½ ounces bittersweet chocolate, chopped

¼ cup heavy cream

CARDAMOM CREAM

½ cup heavy cream

2 tablespoons packed brown sugar

½ teaspoon ground cardamom

✦ Preheat the oven to 300°F. Butter four 6-ounce ramekins.

✦ In a small saucepan, bring the water and the ¼ cup sugar to a boil over medium-high heat; remove from heat.

✦ In a medium bowl, combine the bittersweet chocolate, unsweetened chocolate, and butter.

✦ Pour the sugar mixture over the chocolate mixture and stir until the chocolate and butter melt; set aside.

✦ In a large bowl, using an electric mixer on high speed, beat the egg and the ¾ tablespoon sugar together for 3 minutes, or until pale and thick enough so that the mixture forms a ribbon on the surface when the beater is lifted. Using a rubber spatula, fold the egg mixture into the chocolate mixture.

✦ Place the prepared ramekins in a baking dish just large enough to hold them. Divide the batter among the ramekins and transfer the baking dish to the oven. Add hot water to come three-fourths of the way up the sides of the ramekins. Bake in the preheated oven for 30 minutes, or until a skewer inserted in the center of a cake comes out almost clean. Remove from the oven and let the cakes cool to room temperature, about 30 minutes.

(continued)

✦ While the cakes are baking, make the chocolate sauce: In a small saucepan, combine the chocolate and cream. Stir constantly over low heat until the chocolate melts. Remove from heat and let cool for at least 30 minutes.

✦ To make the cardamom cream: In a chilled bowl, using an electric mixer on high speed, beat the cream, brown sugar, and cardamom together until stiff peaks form; refrigerate until ready to serve.

✦ To serve, unmold the ramekins and place a cake on each plate. Spoon some cardamom cream onto the cakes, drizzle with chocolate sauce, and serve at once.

Makes 4 individual cakes

It isn't where you come from; it's where you're going that counts.

—ELLA FIZGERALD

CAFÉ BOULUD

New York, New York

Chef Daniel Boulud grew up on his family's farm just outside Lyon, France. The town locals met at Café Boulud, a "petit café and not-quite restaurant" that was run by his great-grandparents, grandparents, and parents. When Daniel left home to study haute cuisine at some of the greatest restaurants in France, he carried with him the dream of creating a restaurant that would capture the warmth of that café. The realization of his dream is Café Boulud, located in the former home of Daniel, his first restaurant in New York. This is Boulud's version of a neighborhood café, though here the neighborhood is the ultraluxe Upper East Side of Manhattan.

At his café, Boulud serves the cuisine he grew up with, using American ingredients and techniques he learned in some of the world's best kitchens. To keep things fresh and exciting, and to satisfy his ongoing curiosity about food and flavor, he is also exploring many of the great culinary traditions of the world. By brainstorming with the international cadre of chefs in his kitchen, Boulud is constantly learning and continually inspired to conceive new dishes. It's impossible for patrons to be bored with the food at Café Boulud.

Chef Boulud has divided the restaurant's menu into four sections. La Tradition preserves the rich gastronomic heritage of France and updates classic French dishes. La Saison celebrates seasonal market specialties such as mushrooms from Oregon, seafood from Maine, and the many varieties of vegetables from California gardens. Le Potager places vegetarian offerings at center stage. Boulud loves vegetables and uses classic cooking techniques to emphasize their natural character and flavor. Le Voyage offers both authentic representations and creative renditions of dishes from many of the world's great cuisines. The menu tells the story of Boulud's gastronomic past and allows him to continue his exploration of food and flavor.

As executive chef at restaurant Daniel, Boulud was named Chef of the Year by *Bon Appétit* magazine, and the *International Herald Tribune* named Daniel "one of the ten best restaurants in the world." In 2001, the *New York*

Times awarded Daniel a coveted four-star rating. In addition to Café Boulud, the chef also runs DB Bistro Moderne in New York City and Palm Beach.

Daniel Boulud loves jazz and after work often goes to New York City jazz clubs. This seems entirely natural given the chef's sense of adventure and his love of improvising in the kitchen. The following recipes were chosen to create a vegetarian menu in honor of the great jazz drummer Lewis Nash. Boulud believes that vegetarian meals deserve the very best cooking and often says that seasonal fresh vegetables are his greatest inspiration.

The cooking at Café Boulud achieves almost perfect balance almost all the time. A real rarity, this extraordinary café is beyond compare.

Menu

Chestnut, Celery Root, and Apple Soup

~

Stuffed Romaine Lettuce in Red Wine

~

Potato Gratin Forestier

~

Coffee-Cardamom Pots de Crème

CHESTNUT, CELERY ROOT, AND APPLE SOUP

A delicate-flavored cold-weather soup that makes a perfect first course for Thanksgiving or Christmas dinner. Serve with a light, lively Riesling wine. The soup can made 3 to 4 days before you plan to serve it. Let cool, cover, and refrigerate. Just before serving, bring the soup to a boil.

2 tablespoons extra-virgin olive oil

1 onion, thinly sliced

1 leek, white part only, thinly sliced, washed and dried

2 McIntosh apples, peeled, cored, and cut into ½-inch cubes

10 ounces celery root, peeled and cut into ½-inch cubes (about 2 cups)

1 bay leaf

1 sprig fresh thyme

Pinch of freshly grated nutmeg

Salt and ground white pepper to taste

1¼ pounds chestnuts, peeled (see Basics) or 12 ounces dry-packed, jarred chestnuts

8 cups chicken stock or vegetable stock (see Basics) or canned low-salt chicken broth

½ cup heavy cream

✦ In a large soup pot or casserole, heat the olive oil over medium heat and sauté the onion, leek, apples, celery root, bay leaf, thyme, nutmeg, salt, and pepper for 10 minutes, or until the onion and leeks are soft but not browned. Add the chestnuts and stock or broth and bring to a boil. Reduce heat to low and simmer, skimming the surface occasionally, for 35 minutes, or until the chestnuts can be mashed easily with a fork. Add the cream and simmer for 10 minutes. Discard the bay leaf and thyme.

✦ Using a food processor or hand-held immersion blender, purée the soup. Pour through a fine-mesh sieve into a saucepan. Just before serving, bring the soup back to a boil. *Makes about 4 servings*

At least one day out of the year all musicians should just put their instruments down, and give thanks to Duke Ellington.

—MILES DAVIS

STUFFED ROMAINE LETTUCE IN RED WINE

This satisfying dish requires a lot of preparation, but the root-vegetable stuffed lettuce leaves in a reduction of red wine and port are absolutely delicious.

STUFFING

5 white mushrooms, stemmed

1½ turnips, peeled and coarsely
   chopped

1 small carrot, peeled and coarsely
   chopped

½ large parsnip, peeled and coarsely
   chopped

½ small celery root, peeled and
   coarsely chopped

1 tablespoon unsalted butter

½ large onion, finely chopped

Salt and freshly ground white pepper

2 fresh sage leaves, stemmed and
   minced (stems reserved)

RED WINE SAUCE

1 tablespoon extra-virgin olive oil

Reserved chopped vegetables, onion,
   and sage stems (from above)

Salt and freshly ground white pepper

2½ cups dry red wine

½ cup ruby port

ROMAINE LETTUCE

4 small heads romaine lettuce

Salt and freshly ground white pepper

½ tablespoon unsalted butter

✦ To make the stuffing: In a food processor, combine the mushrooms, turnips, carrot, parsnip, and celery root. Pulse on and off until the vegetables are coarsely chopped into ½-inch pieces.

✦ In a large sauté pan, melt the butter over medium heat and sauté two-thirds of the onion for 5 minutes, or until soft but not browned. Add two-thirds of the chopped vegetables (the remaining vegetables will be used in the sauce), the salt, and pepper and sauté for 10 minutes, or until the vegetables are tender but not browned. Remove from heat and stir in the sage leaves. Let cool.

✦ To make the sauce: In a medium saucepan, heat the olive oil over medium heat and sauté the reserved onion for 5 minutes, or until soft but not browned. Add the reserved vegetables and reserved sage stems and season with salt and pepper to taste. Sauté for 5 minutes. Pour in the wine and port and bring to a boil. Reduce heat to medium and simmer for 45 minutes, or until the liquid reduces to 1 cup.

(continued)

✦ Strain the sauce through a fine-mesh sieve into a saucepan, pressing on the solids with the back of a large spoon to extract as much liquid as possible. Discard the solids and set the saucepan aside.

✦ To make the romaine lettuce: Preheat the oven to 375°F. Generously butter an 8-inch square baking dish.

✦ Discard any tough outer romaine leaves. In a large pot of salted boiling water, blanch the heads of lettuce for 3 minutes, or until the ribs are pliable. Using a wire-mesh skimmer, scoop out the romaine heads and run them under cold water to stop the cooking process.

✦ Using your hands, squeeze each romaine head to get rid of some of the excess water. Cut off and discard the bottom 2 inches of each head and pat the leaves dry between layers of towels. Unroll each head of lettuce and unfold and spread out the leaves; discard the small inner leaves. Cut the layered leaves of each head into a rough square shape and sprinkle with salt and pepper to taste.

✦ Scoop up a generously rounded tablespoonful of stuffing and use the palm of your hand to slightly compact the ball. Place a ball of stuffing near the base of each of the lettuce squares.

✦ Fold up the lettuce leaves around the stuffing to make a packet and cut off any leaves or ribs that do not fold into the ball.

✦ Wrap each packet in a kitchen towel and twist the ends of the towel to squeeze out excess moisture and to make each packet rounder and more uniform in shape. Unwrap the packets and place them, seam side down, in the prepared dish. Spoon the red wine sauce over and cover with a piece of parchment paper cut to fit inside the dish; lightly press the parchment down against the packets. Bake in the preheated oven for 45 minutes. Remove from the oven and transfer the lettuce packets to a warmed platter; loosely cover with aluminum foil to keep warm.

✦ Pour the red wine sauce from the baking dish into a small saucepan. Boil over medium-high heat until the sauce reduces by half. Remove from heat and swirl in the remaining 1 tablespoon butter.

✦ To serve, arrange 2 stuffed romaine lettuces on each of 2 warmed plates, spoon the sauce over, and serve immediately. *Makes 2 servings*

POTATO GRATIN FORESTIER

Gratinéed with Parmesan cheese, this soft, custardy potato-mushroom casserole is a favorite of chef Daniel Boulud.

1 tablespoon unsalted butter

8 ounces assorted mushrooms

Salt and freshly ground white pepper, to taste

Pinch of minced fresh thyme

1 garlic clove, minced

1½ cups heavy cream

Freshly grated nutmeg to taste

2 pounds russet potatoes, peeled

2 tablespoons grated Parmesan cheese

✦ In a medium sauté pan, melt the butter over medium heat and sauté the mushrooms for 3 to 4 minutes, or until tender but not browned. Season with salt and pepper. Transfer the mushrooms to a large bowl and stir in the thyme and garlic. Set aside at room temperature.

✦ Preheat the oven to 350°F. Butter the bottom and sides of an ovenproof 10-inch sauté pan or skillet.

✦ In a large bowl, whisk together the cream, nutmeg, and a generous amount of salt and pepper. Using a mandoline, food processor, or sharp knife, cut the potatoes into very thin rounds and immediately add them to the cream mixture.

✦ Using your hands, pull enough potato slices out of the cream to make a single layer on the bottom of the prepared pan, arranging the potatoes in slightly overlapping concentric circles. Add a second layer of potato slices and pour some cream over. Press down to compact the layers; some of the cream will rise up between the slices. Spread the mushrooms (without any liquid that may have accumulated in the bowl) over the potatoes. Pour more cream over and use your hands to again press down on the ingredients and bring the cream to the top.

✦ Arrange the remaining potatoes in layers over the mushrooms, continuing to pour in cream and press down as you finish each layer. You may not need all of the cream. Sprinkle the top layer evenly with Parmesan cheese. Place the gratin on a baking sheet lined with aluminum foil. Bake in the preheated oven for 45 minutes, or until golden brown. If the gratin is getting too brown, reduce the temperature to 300°F. Bake 15 minutes longer, or until a knife easily pierces all the layers. Remove from the oven and set aside for about 20 minutes before slicing the gratin into wedges. *Makes 3 to 4 side-dish servings*

COFFEE-CARDAMOM POTS DE CRÈME

Rich, creamy custards that perfectly blend the flavors of coffee and cardamom. The inspiration for this elegant dessert was the traditional manner of drinking coffee in some Middle Eastern countries: through a cardamom pod held in one's teeth. Delicious served with a deluxe cream sherry.

½ cup coffee beans, preferably
   espresso roast
1 tablespoon green cardamom pods*
¼ cup plus 2 tablespoons sugar

½ cup whole milk
1 cup heavy cream
3 large egg yolks

✦ In a food processor or coffee grinder, combine the coffee beans and cardamom pods and pulse or grind to coarsely chop.

✦ Transfer the chopped beans and pods to a medium saucepan. Add ¼ cup of the sugar. Place over medium heat and stir constantly until the sugar caramelizes to a mahogany brown. Standing away from the stove, carefully and gradually pour in the milk and ½ cup of the cream. The caramel will immediately seize and harden but will smooth out as it warms and the sugar melts again. When the sugar has melted and the mixture is smooth again, remove from heat. Cover the pan with a lid and let stand for 20 minutes.

✦ Preheat the oven to 300°F. In a large bowl, whisk the egg yolks and the remaining 2 tablespoons sugar together until pale and thick. Strain the coffee mixture through a fine-mesh sieve into a measuring cup; discard the beans and pods. Add enough of the remaining ½ cup heavy cream to bring the liquid to 1 cup. In order to avoid air bubbles, very gradually and gently stir the liquid into the egg mixture.

✦ Arrange 4 pot de crème pots or custard cups or 6 espresso cups in a small baking dish and fill each cup with the custard. Fill the baking dish with hot water to come halfway up the sides of the cups and bake in the preheated oven for 45 minutes, or until the custards are set but still jiggle in the center when shaken.

✦ Remove from the oven and let the custards sit in the water bath for 10 minutes. Lift the cups out of the water and let cool. Cover and refrigerate for at least 1 hour or up to 24 hours. Bring the custards to room temperature before serving. *Makes 4 to 6 individual custards*

*Available at some supermarkets, Indian markets, and specialty foods stores (see Glossary and Resources).

CASANOVA
Carmel, California

Known as Carmel's most romantic restaurant, Casanova has been delighting Carmel residents and out-of-town visitors since 1977. The restaurant's owners, Walter, Denise, and Gaston Georis and Michel Mignon, grew up in the same small town in Belgium. All four eventually immigrated to the United States and settled in Carmel. One evening, after realizing that they were all homesick for Europe's wonderful country restaurants, the group decided to open a small bistro. They wanted to create a place where guests could enjoy great food, a glass of wine, and an espresso in the company of good friends. After their first restaurant, La Bohème, outgrew its space, they opened Casanova. Such innovations as fresh pasta, excellent bread, and real espresso were unusual at the time, as was the contemporary European music that played in the dining room.

In fact, for at least two of Casanova's owners, music was important long before the restaurant business. Along with John Blakeley, Walter and Gaston Georis played in the sixties-era band The Sandals. Visitors to Casanova can sometimes hear their music CDs at the restaurant.

Casanova is situated just off Carmel's Ocean Avenue in a building that was once owned by Charlie Chaplin's cook, known as Aunt Fairy Bird. Walter Georis designed the restaurant and its interior, inspired by childhood memories of his grandparents' Belgian farmhouse. Charming gardens and an alfresco dining area were added, and a wine cellar under the restaurant was excavated by hand.

Casanova's menu highlights southern French, Spanish, and northern Italian flavors. Included with each entrée are starters such as olives, sun-dried tomato tapenade, and fresh-baked bread, as well as an appetizer chosen from the menu. The wine cellar houses about thirty thousand bottles, and Casanova consistently wins the Grand Award of Excellence from *Wine Spectator* magazine.

The largest of Casanova's three dining areas, the Harvest Room, is a traditional French Provençal room surrounded by lavender- and rose-filled planters. The Milagro Room is decorated in the style of an Alpine chalet, and the Van Gogh Room was specially built to house the table where Vincent Van Gogh dined at the Auberge Ravoux. The Auberge was Van Gogh's favorite restaurant in Auvers-sur-Oise, an artists' village just outside Paris. Walter Georis visited the restaurant, which is now also a Van Gogh museum, and made friends with the owners over a six-hour meal. To cement the friendship, the owners presented Georis with Van Gogh's table for Casanova restaurant.

Carmel is just a few miles from Monterey, home of the Monterey Jazz Festival. Every year, some of the world's greatest jazz musicians gather in Monterey for a three-day celebration of nonstop music. For visitors to the jazz festival, or for travelers enjoying California's stunning coastal scenery, dinner at Casanova offers just what the owners first envisioned: a beautiful setting in which to enjoy good company, great food, and fine wine. Didier Dutertre, who has been the chef at Casanova for over twenty years, created the following recipes and presented them to Menus and Music.

The first thing we must keep in mind about a musician is that the music he plays is a reflection of his true self . . . You are what you are; that is reality, you can't escape it. And the reality of the musician—especially the jazz musician—is that the music is a continuance of himself.

—DIZZY GILLESPIE

Menu

Warm Asparagus Citronette

~

Lamb Brochettes with Thyme and Moroccan-Style Rice

~

Caramelized Apples with Vanilla Bean Ice Cream and Caramel Sauce

WARM ASPARAGUS CITRONETTE

1 small bunch fresh asparagus, trimmed

1 teaspoon fresh lemon juice

1 teaspoon Dijon mustard

Salt and freshly ground pepper to taste

3 tablespoons extra-virgin olive oil

✦ Peel the asparagus stalks.

✦ In a small bowl, whisk the lemon juice, Dijon mustard, salt, and pepper together. Gradually whisk in the olive oil until emulsified and set the citronette aside.

✦ In a large pot of salted boiling water, cook the asparagus for 3 to 4 minutes, or until crisp-tender. Drain the asparagus and immediately plunge them into a bowl of ice water to stop the cooking process. Drain the asparagus and transfer them to a serving plate. Drizzle the citronette over the top. *Makes 2 servings*

LAMB BROCHETTES WITH THYME AND MOROCCAN-STYLE RICE

This dish is also delicious with grilled marinated lamb chops made in the same manner as the brochettes.

2 garlic cloves, crushed

1 tablespoon olive oil

Leaves from 1 fresh thyme sprig

Salt and freshly ground pepper to taste

12 ounces boneless leg of lamb, cut
    into 1-inch cubes

1 onion, cut into eighths

Moroccan-Style Rice (recipe follows)

✦ Light a fire in a charcoal grill. Soak 2 wooden skewers in water for 30 minutes. Alternatively, preheat a broiler.

✦ In a medium bowl, stir the garlic, olive oil, thyme, salt, and pepper together. Add the lamb and toss until the lamb is well coated; set aside.

✦ Alternately thread the meat and onion pieces onto the skewers. Grill or broil for about 3 minutes on each side. Sprinkle with salt to taste. Serve over Moroccan-style rice. *Makes 2 servings*

MOROCCAN-STYLE RICE

2 cups chicken stock (see Basics) or
    canned low-salt chicken broth
2 tablespoons olive oil
1 small onion, finely chopped
1 cup long-grain white rice
1 carrot, finely diced
1 bay leaf
1 fresh thyme sprig

Salt to taste
1 tablespoon *each* raisins and dried
    currants, soaked in hot water until
    plump and drained
1 teaspoon unsalted butter
½ cup blanched fresh English peas or
    thawed frozen peas
1 tablespoon slivered almonds

✦ Preheat the oven to 375°F. In a small saucepan, bring the chicken stock or broth to a boil over medium-high heat; set aside.

✦ In a large, ovenproof pot, heat the olive oil over medium-low heat, and sauté the onion for 7 minutes, or until golden. Add the rice and stir for 2 minutes, or until opaque. Add the carrot, broth or stock, bay leaf, thyme, salt, raisins, and currants. Bring to a boil, cover, and bake in the preheated oven for 20 minutes. Remove from the oven and let rest for 5 minutes before taking off the lid. Gently stir in the butter, peas, and almonds. Season with salt and pepper to taste and transfer to a serving bowl. Serve warm. *Makes about 3 cups*

CARAMELIZED APPLES WITH
VANILLA BEAN ICE CREAM AND CARAMEL SAUCE

A simple and utterly satisfying dessert.

1 teaspoon unsalted butter

2 tablespoon sugar

2 large Fuji or Golden Delicious
   apples, peeled, cored, and
   left whole

CARAMEL SAUCE

¼ cup sugar

1 teaspoon water

½ teaspoon fresh lemon juice

2 tablespoons heavy cream

1 tablespoon unsalted butter

Vanilla Bean Ice Cream
   (for homemade see page 57)

✦ In a sauté pan, melt the butter over medium heat. Stir in the sugar and cook until golden brown, about 5 minutes. Add the whole apples and cook, turning them over every 5 minutes or so, for 15 to 20 minutes, or until soft.

✦ To make the caramel sauce: In a small saucepan, cook the sugar, water, and lemon juice over medium-high heat until amber colored, about 15 minutes. Remove from heat and stir in the cream and butter; set aside and keep warm.

✦ To serve, place an apple on each of 2 plates and top with a scoop of vanilla ice cream. Pour the caramel over the top and serve at once. *Makes 2 servings*

CASTLE HILL INN AND RESORT
Newport, Rhode Island

Situated on a pristine forty-acre peninsula off Newport's renowned Ocean Drive, Castle Hill offers the romance, seclusion, and extraordinary beauty of a historic oceanfront estate. The Victorian-era mansion has expansive rolling lawns with breathtaking views of Narragansett Bay, luxurious guest accommodations, and four dining rooms in which to enjoy exceptional cuisine.

The Castle Hill mansion was built in 1874 as a summer retreat for Alexander Agassiz, a scientist who decided that Newport was a perfect place to study marine biology. A few years later, Agassiz built a research laboratory on the property in a chalet style reminiscent of his native Switzerland. The laboratory was later turned into a guest cottage and used as a summer home by the owners of Castle Hill until it became part of the Inn in the 1980s. Today the Inn and Resort includes the Agassiz Mansion, the Chalet, the Harbor House rooms, and the Beach House rooms, which are just steps away from a private beach. All the accommodations are nests of comfort that retain the quiet and charm of nineteenth-century seacoast life.

Guests at Castle Hill can enjoy the illustrious Newport Jazz Festival, which takes place every August. Founded in 1954 by George Wein, the Newport Jazz Festival was the first outdoor music festival devoted entirely to jazz. Other nearby attractions include the Cliffwalk, Brenton Point State Park, and The Preservation Society tours of historic mansion such as The Breakers, the Vanderbilt's lavish summer escape.

The following recipes were created by chef Casey Riley, who uses the best regional, seasonal ingredients and also finds inspiration in international seasonings and tastes. Riley relies on the local fishing fleet and private growers from Maine to the Chesapeake for the freshest seafood, meats, and produce. His complex dishes often have delicious Caribbean, Asian, Native American, French, and Mediterranean influences. The restaurant's extensive wine list has been carefully chosen to complement Riley's cooking. Including more than five hundred selections, it has received the *Wine Spectator* magazine's Award of Excellence. Castle Hill is a gorgeous setting for special occasion dining, and chef Casey Riley says, "With the sunset and the views, I want to make the food as romantic as the setting."

MENU

ROASTED PUMPKIN AND CHEDDAR SOUP
WITH SPICED, CARAMELIZED PEARS

~

BUTTER-ROASTED LOBSTER WITH
A WHITE TRUFFLE SOUFFLÉ AND ROASTED CORN SAUCE

~

VANILLA BEAN SORBET WITH
MANGO AND KIWI PURÉES AND CASHEW TUILES

Roasted Pumpkin and Cheddar Soup with Spiced, Caramelized Pears

A perfect soup for Thanksgiving dinner or for any special autumn meal.

Spice Mixture
1 teaspoon *each* light brown sugar, chili powder, ground sage, cinnamon, nutmeg, coriander, and cardamom

1 small sugar pumpkin, halved top to bottom and seeded
4 tablespoons unsalted butter, cut into 4 pieces
2 cups dry white wine
2 tablespoons canola oil
½ onion, diced

3 garlic cloves, minced
1 potato, peeled and quartered
2 cups chicken stock (see Basics), canned low-salt chicken broth, or water
2 cups (8 ounces) shredded white Cheddar cheese
Fresh lemon juice, salt, white pepper, and light brown sugar to taste
1 Bartlett pear, peeled, cored, and diced
1 tablespoon granulated sugar
Sage leaves for garnish (optional)

✦ In a small bowl, combine all the spice mixture ingredients. Stir to blend. Reserve a pinch of spice for the pears and set the rest aside.

✦ Preheat the oven to 350°F. Place the pumpkin on a baking sheet, cut side up. Sprinkle the cavities evenly with the spice mixture. Add 2 tablespoons of the butter and ½ cup of the wine to each cavity. Bake in the preheated oven for 45 minutes to 60 minutes, or until very tender. Let cool slightly. Pour off and reserve any liquid from the cavities. Peel off the skin and cut the pumpkin into large pieces.

✦ While the pumpkin is roasting, heat 1 tablespoon of the canola oil in a soup pot over medium heat. Sauté the onion until lightly browned. Add the garlic and sauté for 2 minutes. Add the potato and 1 cup wine and cook until the wine reduces by half. Add the stock, broth, or water and simmer until the potato is tender.

✦ Add the pumpkin and the reserved roasting liquid. Transfer the mixture to a food processor or blender, add the cheese, and purée. Season the soup with lemon, salt, pepper, and a little brown sugar.

✦ In a small sauté pan, heat the remaining canola oil over high heat and sauté the pear, sugar, and reserved spice mix until browned. Sprinkle the caramelized pear over the soup. Serve garnished with a sage leaf, if desired. *Makes 6 servings*

BUTTER-ROASTED LOBSTER WITH A WHITE TRUFFLE SOUFFLÉ AND ROASTED CORN SAUCE

Delicious served with roasted autumn squash or tomatoes. To simplify this dish, make it without the soufflé.

1 tablespoon pickling spice
1 tablespoon Old Bay seasoning
1 lemon, halved
Salt to taste
Two live lobsters
4 tablespoons cold unsalted butter
⅓ cup dry white wine

WHITE TRUFFLE SOUFFLÉS
½ potato, peeled and cut into pieces
½ ounce fresh white truffle or
   1 tablespoon white truffle purée*

½ tablespoon heavy cream
½ tablespoon cold unsalted butter,
   cut into small pieces
2 ounces Brie cheese, rind cut off
2 eggs, separated
Salt to taste, plus 1 teaspoon
Freshly ground white pepper to taste
Pinch of cornstarch

Roasted Corn Sauce (recipe follows)
Minced fresh chives for garnish
   (optional)

✦ Fill a large stockpot two-thirds full with water. Add the pickling spice, Old Bay seasoning, lemon, and salt; cover and bring to a boil. Add the lobsters. Bring back to a boil and cook for 5 minutes. Pull out the lobsters and transfer to an ice water bath for a few minutes to stop the cooking process.

✦ Once cooled, remove the claws and knuckles in one piece and remove the tail from the body. Separate the claw and knuckle at the joint. Using the dull edge of a knife, crack the bottom half of the claw and break off the shell, leaving the claw meat on the top half of the shell.

✦ Rinse away any white coagulated material with warm water. Using kitchen scissors, cut open the shell of the knuckles lengthwise and pull out the meat. For the tails, press them flat and cut all the way through the shell to cut in half. Remove the intestinal vein on the bottom of the tail. Rinse the meat lightly in warm water. Reserve the knuckle meat for the soufflé.

✦ Preheat the oven to 400°F. Place the lobster tails in a baking dish, shell side down, and place 1 tablespoon butter on each piece. Place the claws on top and drizzle the white wine over. Set aside.

✦ To make the soufflés: Preheat the oven to 400°F. Butter two 6-ounce ramekins.

✦ In a medium saucepan, cook the potato in salted boiling water until tender, about 10 minutes. Drain. Pass the potato through a food mill or lightly mash.

✦ In a food processor, add the fresh truffle and purée. In a medium saucepan, combine the truffle purée, cream, and butter. Bring to a simmer over medium-low heat. Stir in the potato and Brie and remove from heat. Let cool to body temperature then whisk in the egg yolks. Season with salt and pepper .

✦ In a medium bowl, using an electric mixer, beat the egg whites with the 1 teaspoon salt and the cornstarch until soft peaks form. Gently fold the whites into the potato mixture; do not stir (thin streaks of white are fine). Spoon into the prepared ramekins. Place the lobster in the preheated oven along with the soufflés. Bake the lobster for 5 minutes, or until heated through, and the soufflés for 12 minutes, or until puffed and golden.

✦ To serve, immediately and gently unmold a soufflé onto each of 2 warmed plates. Interlock the tail halves and place them on top of the soufflé. Lean the claws against the soufflé and ladle the sauce on one side of the plate. Garnish with chives, if desired, and serve at once. *Makes 2 servings*

*Available at specialty foods stores and some supermarkets (see Resources).

Roasted Corn Sauce

2 ears unshucked corn, roasted in a
   preheated 350°F oven for 30 minutes
½ cup dry white wine
1 tablespoon canola oil
½ small sweet white onion, such as
   Vidalia, sliced very thin
½ vanilla bean, split lengthwise

½ jalapeño chili*, seeded and minced
1 garlic clove, minced
1 tablespoon brandy
Fresh lemon juice, salt, and white
   pepper to taste
2 tablespoons cold unsalted butter

(continued)

✦ Shuck the corn and cut off the kernels. In a medium saucepan, simmer the corn and white wine over medium heat for 10 minutes. Transfer to a food processor or blender and purée.

✦ In a medium saucepan, heat the canola oil over medium heat and sauté the onion for 3 minutes, or until translucent. Add the vanilla bean, chili, and garlic and sauté for 3 minutes. Add the brandy and cook to reduce by half. Add the corn purée and simmer for 30 minutes. Remove the vanilla bean. Season with lemon, salt, and pepper. Remove from heat. Whisk in the cold butter and serve warm.

Makes about 1½ cups

*Available at many produce stores and supermarkets (see Glossary).

VANILLA BEAN SORBET WITH
MANGO AND KIWI PURÉES AND CASHEW TUILES

This sorbet makes a delightfully light and refreshing dessert served with colorful fruit purées and delicate, roof-tile shaped cookies.

1 cup sugar

2 cups water

1 tablespoon fresh lemon juice

1 vanilla bean, split lengthwise

MANGO AND KIWI PURÉES

1 ripe mango, peeled and diced
   (see Basics)

2 ripe kiwis, peeled and diced

Cashew Tuiles (recipe follows)

✦ In a medium saucepan, combine the sugar, 1 cup of the water, and the lemon juice. Bring to a boil over high heat. Reduce heat to low and add the vanilla bean to the pan. Bring to a simmer. Remove from heat and let cool to room temperature. The longer the mixture is set aside to infuse, the more intense the vanilla flavor will be.

✦ Strain the liquid through a fine-mesh sieve into a bowl. Add the remaining 1 cup water and refrigerate for at least 2 hours. Freeze in an ice cream maker according to the manufacturer's instructions.

✦ To make the purées: Separately purée the mango and kiwi in a food processor or blender. Transfer each purée to a bowl, cover, and refrigerate.

(continued)

All a musician can do is get closer to the sources of nature, and so feel that he is in communion with the natural laws.

—JOHN COLTRANE

CASHEW TUILES

¼ cup powdered sugar

¼ cup all-purpose flour

3 tablespoons unsalted butter at room
temperature

2 tablespoons honey

3 tablespoons egg white

1 cup (4 ounces) unsalted cashews,
lightly toasted (see Basics), salted,
and finely chopped

✦ Preheat the oven to 350°F. Line a baking sheet with a silpat or buttered
parchment paper.

✦ In a medium bowl, stir the sugar and flour together.

✦ In a medium bowl, using an electric mixer, beat the butter and honey together
until pale and fluffy. With the mixer on low, add the flour mixture. Gradually add
the egg white. Beat on high speed for about 10 seconds, or until just combined.

✦ Spoon the batter by tablespoonfuls 1½ inches apart onto the prepared baking
sheet. Generously sprinkle with cashews. Bake in the preheated oven for 5 to
6 minutes, or until golden. Watch carefully, because the tuiles can brown quickly.
Remove from the oven and quickly remove the cookies, using a thin metal spatula.
Immediately drape each one over a rolling pin until cool and firm. *Makes about
15 tuiles*

COMMANDER'S PALACE
New Orleans, Louisiana

One of the grand old restaurants of New Orleans, Commander's Palace has propelled Creole cuisine into the American mainstream over the years and has launched the careers of more than two dozen chefs, including Paul Prudhomme, Emeril Lagasse, and Jamie Shannon. Today chef Tory McPhail keeps the energy flowing with exciting new dishes and fresh, sophisticated reinterpretations of traditional Creole dishes. Since 1974, the restaurant has been kept in top form by the exacting standards of two generations of Brennan women. Ella Brennan, the matriarch of the Brennan family, says: "Our business is to make people happy," and the warm, spirited personalities of the Brennan clan fill the restaurant with *joie de vivre* and Southern hospitality.

Famed for its celebratory dinners and gala Sunday jazz brunches, Commander's Palace is located in the Garden District, just across from the historic Lafayette Cemetery No. 1 immortalized by author Anne Rice. The mansion is an aqua-and-white Victorian fantasy of turrets, columns, and gingerbread trim. Its ambiance is a unique New Orleansian blend of down-to-earth comfort and historic opulence. To reach some areas of the restaurant, guests are led to their seats through the kitchen, breaking down the barrier between the dining room and the heart of the restaurant. Even the bar is located in the kitchen so that patrons can watch the cooking brigade while enjoying a cocktail. Servers wear bistro aprons over starched shirts and are renowned for their graciousness. Commander's Palace has received numerous awards, including the James Beard Foundation Lifetime Outstanding Restaurant Award.

The following recipes were created by Tory McPhail, who became executive chef after a stint at the Las Vegas Commander's Palace. McPhail is creating new dishes and re-interpreting haute Creole classics to make the food more energetic than ever. He points out that 90 percent of the ingredients he uses come from within 100 miles of the restaurant's back door, including fresh seafood and organic produce from local farmers. Deeply rooted in the Big Easy culture, Creole cuisine combines French, Spanish, Native American, and Afro-Caribbean influences.

A special menu is served for the jazz brunch on Saturdays and Sundays, when two bands rove through the restaurant after performing for the chefs in the kitchen. Brightly colored balloons, flowers, fine wines, and splendid food combined with live Dixieland jazz create a world-class dining experience, New Orleans style.

Commander's Palace has been in continuous operation since it was opened by Emile Commander in the early 1880s. It hasn't remained a legend by resting on its laurels, and it's easy to see why "the city that never stops eating" hasn't stopped dining at Commander's Palace for the past 122 years. *Laissez roulez le bon temps*—let the good times roll!

We're still listening to the propulsion that was behind the mind that sent forth Kind of Blue *and* Blue Train. *We're not done with the music from that time. We'll never be done with that. Miles was like an Impressionist. You don't have to ask "Is it John Coltrane?" Same with Miles.*

—TAJ MAHAL

Menu

Gumbo YaYa

~

Crusted Pork Tenderloin

~

Bread Pudding Soufflé with Bourbon Custard Sauce

Gumbo YaYa

Thick, meaty, and suffused with spice, this classic gumbo is served with boiled white rice. Commander Palace chef Tory McPhail adjusts the consistency of the gumbo seasonally, serving his gumbo thick in colder weather and thinner during the warmer months.

1 pound chicken pieces

Salt and freshly ground pepper to taste

Flour for dredging, plus ¼ cup
   all-purpose flour

¼ cup canola or peanut oil

1 onion, diced

3 celery stalks, diced

2 green bell peppers, seeded, deribbed,
   and diced

6 garlic cloves, minced

½ teaspoon cayenne pepper, or
   to taste

Pinch *each* of dried oregano, basil,
   and thyme

2 bay leaves

4 cups cold water

1 large andouille sausage* (about
   12 ounces), cut into slices ½ inch
   thick

½ tablespoon filé powder*

½ tablespoon hot sauce, or to taste

2 cups boiled rice (see Basics)

2 scallions, including green parts,
   thinly sliced

✦ Sprinkle the chicken with salt and pepper and dredge lightly in flour.

✦ In a large, heavy pot, heat the canola or peanut oil over medium-high heat until almost smoking. Sear the chicken until golden brown, about 5 minutes on the first side and 4 minutes on the second side. Using tongs, transfer the chicken to a plate.

✦ Heat the oil in the same pan over medium-high heat until smoking. Gradually stir in the ¼ cup flour to make a roux. Stir constantly for 3 to 5 minutes, or until the roux is the color of milk chocolate. Do not burn.

✦ Add the onion and stir for 1 minute. Add the celery and stir for 30 seconds. Add the bell peppers and stir for 1 minute. Add the garlic, cayenne, oregano, basil, thyme, bay leaves, and salt and pepper to taste. Gradually add the water, stirring constantly to prevent lumps.

✦ Stir in the chicken and sausage and bring to a boil. Reduce heat to low and simmer, uncovered, for about 2 hours, skimming off any fat that rises to the top. When the meat is falling off the bones, remove the chicken from the pot and pull it off the bones; return the meat to the pot and bring to a boil. Adjust the consistency of the gumbo by adding water or further reducing the liquid. Remove from heat and stir in the filé until it is dissolved. Add the hot sauce, taste, and adjust the seasoning. Serve over rice and sprinkle with scallions. *Makes 6 to 8 servings*

*Available in specialty foods stores and many supermarkets (see Glossary).

CRUSTED PORK TENDERLOIN

4 whole shallots

4 unpeeled garlic cloves

2 tablespoons unsalted butter or olive oil, plus more for coating and drizzling

12 ounces pork tenderloin

Salt and freshly ground pepper to taste

2 tablespoons minced fresh thyme

1 garnet yam or sweet potato, peeled and finely diced

8 cremini mushrooms, quartered

¼ cup dry red wine

1 cup chicken stock (see Basics) or canned low-salt chicken broth

1 handful spinach leaves

1 handful arugula leaves

✦ Preheat the oven to 350°F. Put the shallots and garlic cloves in a small baking dish and dot with butter or drizzle with olive oil. Bake in the preheated oven for 45 minutes, or until soft. Let cool to room temperature. Quarter each shallot and peel the garlic cloves.

✦ Coat the pork tenderloin with butter or olive oil and sprinkle with salt, pepper, and 1 tablespoon of the thyme.

✦ In a large sauté pan over high heat, sear the tenderloin until browned on all sides. Roast in the preheated oven for about 25 minutes, or until an instant-read thermometer inserted into the thickest part of the meat registers 160°F. Remove from the oven and let rest.

✦ Meanwhile, in a large sauté pan, melt the 2 tablespoons butter or heat the olive oil over medium-high heat and sauté the shallot, garlic, yam or sweet potato, and mushrooms for 7 minutes, or until the yam or sweet potato is soft. Season with salt and pepper to taste, pour in the wine, and stir to scrape up any browned bits from the bottom of the pan. Pour in the stock or broth and bring to a simmer. Stir in the spinach, arugula, and the remaining thyme and cook until the spinach wilts.

✦ Slice the pork tenderloin into ½-inch-thick medallions. Spoon a mound of vegetables and a little broth onto each of 2 plates. Arrange the pork slices on top and serve at once. *Makes 2 servings*

Bread Pudding Soufflé with Bourbon Custard Sauce

Perfect for two people to share, this custardy bread pudding is light and fluffy as a soufflé and topped with a silky bourbon sauce. For twenty years, it has been the best-selling dessert at Commander's Palace, which serves as many as three thousand orders a week.

½ cup sugar, plus more for sprinkling
½ teaspoon ground cinnamon
Pinch of freshly grated nutmeg
1 large egg, lightly beaten
½ cup heavy cream
½ teaspoon vanilla extract
2 cups day-old crustless French, Italian,
    or challah bread cubes
3 tablespoons raisins

3 large egg whites at room temperature
Pinch of cream of tartar

Bourbon Custard Sauce

½ cup heavy cream
¾ teaspoon cornstarch dissolved in
    1 tablespoon water
1½ tablespoons sugar
2 tablespoons bourbon

✦ Preheat the oven to 350°F. Butter an 8-by-4-inch loaf pan.

✦ In a large bowl, combine ¼ cup of the sugar, the cinnamon, and nutmeg. Whisk in the egg, cream, and vanilla. Add the bread and let stand for 5 minutes, stirring occasionally until the bread soaks up the liquid.

✦ Scatter the raisins in the bottom of the prepared loaf pan. Spoon in the bread and smooth the top. Bake in the preheated oven for 25 minutes, or until golden brown and a skewer inserted in the center comes out almost clean. Remove from the oven and set aside.

✦ Butter a 3-cup baking dish and sprinkle it with sugar, tapping out the excess.

✦ In a dry, clean bowl, using an electric mixer on medium speed, beat the egg whites with the cream of tartar until frothy. Increase the speed to high and beat until soft peaks form. Gradually add the remaining ¼ cup sugar, beating until stiff, glossy peaks form. Do not over beat or the whites will break down.

✦ Spoon half of the bread pudding into a large bowl and use a spoon or your hands to break it into bite-sized pieces. Fold in one-fourth of the beaten egg whites and spoon this mixture into the bottom of the baking dish. Add the remaining bread pudding to the bowl, break into bite-sized pieces, and fold in the remaining egg whites. Spoon the mixture into the dish, mounding it above the rim. Bake in the preheated oven for 25 minutes, or until golden and puffed.

✦ Meanwhile, make the bourbon sauce: In a small saucepan over medium heat, bring the cream to a boil. Whisk in the cornstarch mixture and cook for 1 minute, or until slightly thickened. Remove from heat and stir in the sugar and bourbon. Return to medium-low heat and simmer for 1 minute. Remove from heat and let cool to room temperature. To make ahead, refrigerate overnight and bring to room temperature before serving.

✦ To serve, use a spoon to poke a hole in the center of the soufflé and pour in half the bourbon sauce. Serve at once, with the remaining sauce alongside. *Makes 2 servings*

40 SARDINES

Overland Park, Kansas

4 0 Sardines is a favorite for stylish Kansas City residents who enjoy American bistro cooking prepared by acclaimed chefs Debbie Gold and Michael Smith. The husband-and-wife team met in the kitchen at Charlie Trotter's restaurant in Chicago, and their dual cooking careers continued at L'Albion in the south of France. During a meal on the Riviera one day, they discussed opening their own restaurant, while Smith consumed forty sardines. Years later when their dream finally came true, the pair named the restaurant after that memorable lunch.

40 Sardines is decorated in a cool blue and green palette that echoes the silvery skin of its namesake. An open kitchen and a large communal table emphasize a friendly, upbeat style, and fresh flowers and votive candles add color and warmth. The sleek bar and dining counter was custom made from a translucent azure compound embedded with white river stones.

Fresh and straightforward, the cuisine at 40 Sardines is influenced by world flavors and based on the chefs' French training. After returning from France, Gold and Smith worked as executive chefs at the American Restaurant in Kansas City, where they were awarded the James Beard Award for Best Chefs in the Midwest. The wine list at 40 Sardines combines excellence with accessibility and has won *Wine Spectator* magazine's Award of Excellence. One popular feature of the list is a menu of twenty bottles at $20; patrons also appreciate the extensive list of wines by the glass and demi-bottles.

Popular restaurant events include Jazzy Sundays, when local musicians perform between 6 and 9 P.M., and on the first Sunday of every month an evening of opera and musical theater is co-sponsored by the Lyric Opera of Kansas City. As longtime members of the culinary industry, Gray and Smith understand that service industry professionals need a break too. Every Monday night at 40 Sardines, any restaurant employee in the Kansas City area can enjoy a three-course meal for just $20. Cooking classes and demonstrations are held at the restaurant throughout the year.

The following recipes were presented to Menus and Music by Debbie Gold and Michael Smith.

Menu

Asparagus and Ramp Salad with
Artichoke Crisps and Mushroom Relish

~

Grilled Sardines with Salsa Verde
and Fingerling Potatoes

~

Thyme- and Garlic-Studded Veal Chops
with Polenta

~

Chocolate-Port Cake

Asparagus and Ramp Salad with Artichoke Crisps and Mushroom Relish

This fresh starter that takes full advantage of spring vegetables. If ramps are unavailable, make the salad with scallions.

MUSHROOM RELISH

1 tablespoon olive oil

4 cremini mushrooms, finely diced

1 small portobello mushroom, stemmed and finely diced

4 shiitake mushrooms, stemmed and finely diced

1 teaspoon minced fresh thyme

2 drops black truffle oil

3 tablespoons sherry vinegar

1 tablespoon minced shallots

1 tablespoon minced fresh chives

Salt and freshly ground pepper to taste

16 asparagus stalks

Salt and freshly ground pepper to taste

5 tablespoons olive oil, plus more for drizzling

6 ramps* or scallions

1 artichoke, trimmed (see Basics)

Canola oil for deep-frying

Juice of ½ lemon

1 small bunch frisée lettuce, stemmed

½ cup arugula leaves

✦ To make the relish: In a large sauté pan over medium-high, heat the olive oil and sauté the mushrooms for 4 to 5 minutes, or until they release their liquid. Remove the pan from heat and stir in the thyme, truffle oil, and vinegar; set aside to cool. Stir in the shallots, chives, salt, and pepper.

✦ In a large pot of salted boiling water, cook the asparagus for 4 minutes, or until crisp-tender. Drain and run under cold water to stop the cooking process; drain again. Transfer the asparagus to a plate and sprinkle with salt, pepper and 2 tablespoons of the olive oil; set aside.

✦ In the same pot of boiling water, blanch the ramps or scallions for 1 minute; drain and set aside.

(continued)

✦ In a heavy, medium saucepan, heat 2 inches of the canola oil over medium-high heat to 365°F, or until it is almost smoking. Thinly slice the artichoke heart and immediately deep-fry the slices until crisp, about 1 minute. Using a slotted spoon, transfer the artichoke slices to paper towels to drain.

✦ To serve, arrange the asparagus and ramps on each of 2 plates. In a small bowl, whisk the remaining 3 tablespoons olive oil, the lemon juice, and salt and pepper together to make a vinaigrette. In a medium bowl, toss the frisée and arugula with the vinaigrette and place a mound of salad at the base of the asparagus and ramps. Sprinkle each plate with some artichoke chips and mushroom relish. Drizzle the plates with olive oil and serve at once. *Makes 2 servings*

*Available at specialty produce stores and farmer's markets (see Glossary and Resources).

I'm saying: to be continued, until we meet again.
Meanwhile, keep on listening and tapping your feet.

—Count Basie

Grilled Sardines with Salsa Verde and Fingerling Potatoes

Sensational flavors combine in this vibrant dish, which even sardine haters will love.

Confit Tomatoes
4 tomatoes

Salsa Verde
½ cup fresh flat-leaf parsley
Leaves from 3 sprigs fresh thyme
Leaves from 2 sprigs fresh tarragon
Leaves from 3 sprigs fresh oregano
½ clove garlic
½ teaspoon red pepper flakes
½ tablespoon capers
1 anchovy

½ cup extra-virgin olive oil
Juice of ½ lemon

4 to 6 fresh sardines
2 tablespoons extra-virgin olive oil,
   plus more for coating
1 garlic clove, minced
Salt and freshly ground pepper to taste
6 fingerling potatoes or other small
   new potatoes
½ bunch watercress, stemmed

✦ To make the confit tomatoes: Preheat the oven to 300°F. In a large saucepan of boiling water, blanch the tomatoes for 15 seconds. Drain and slip off the tomato skins. Cut each tomato in half and lightly squeeze out the seeds and excess juice. Place the tomatoes in a shallow casserole dish, cut side up. Drizzle with olive oil and season with salt and pepper. Bake in the preheated oven for 1½ hours, or until they shrivel and collapse. Remove from the oven and set aside.

✦ To make the salsa verde: In a food processor, combine all the ingredients and process to make a coarse purée; set aside.

✦ Snap off the head of each sardine, pulling away with it most of the intestines. Remove the center back fin and little attached bones by pulling away the fin, starting at the tail end. Open each sardine by slipping your thumbnail into the belly cavity and running it against the spine all the way to the tail. Open the sardine completely flat and lift out the spine, pulling the spine toward the tail.

(continued)

Pull the spine sharply away from the fish, taking the tail with it. Wash the boned, butterflied sardines under cold running water, rinsing away any remaining guts or loose bones. Coat the sardines with olive oil on both sides. Sprinkle with garlic, salt, and pepper; set aside. In a medium pot of salted boiling water, cook the potatoes until tender when pierced with a fork; drain and let cool. Cut each potato in half lengthwise. In a medium bowl, toss the potatoes with the 2 tablespoons olive oil and salt and pepper to taste; set aside.

✦ In a medium bowl, toss the watercress with 2 tablespoons of the salsa verde.

✦ Light a fire in a charcoal grill or preheat a broiler. Grill the sardines, skin side down. Alternatively, broil, flesh side up and 2 to 3 inches from the heat source, for 2 to 3 minutes.

✦ To serve, arrange 3 potatoes in the center of each of 2 plates. Arrange 2 or 3 sardines on each plate. Top the sardines with 2 tomato halves. Garnish each plate with watercress salad and drizzle each plate with salsa verde; serve without delay. *Makes 2 servings*

THYME- AND GARLIC-STUDDED VEAL CHOPS WITH POLENTA

2 thick-cut veal chops
3 tablespoons olive oil
Salt and freshly ground pepper to taste
4 garlic cloves, halved lengthwise
Leaves from 2 sprigs fresh thyme, chopped
½ onion, thinly sliced
8 baby carrots
½ cup dry white wine

2 artichoke hearts (see Basics), quartered
Bouquet garni: 2 sprigs *each* fresh thyme, parsley, and cilantro, plus dried mushrooms, tied in a cheesecloth square
1 tablespoon finely shredded fresh basil leaves
Polenta (recipe follows)

✦ Preheat the oven to 375°F. Using a paring knife, poke 3 small holes into each of the veal chops and insert 3 of the garlic halves. Drizzle the meat with 1 tablespoon of the olive oil and generously season with salt and pepper. Spread the thyme on a plate and roll the veal in it until coated; set aside.

✦ In a large ovenproof sauté pan, heat the remaining 1 tablespoon olive oil over medium heat and sauté the onion and carrots for 5 minutes. Thinly slice the remaining garlic and sauté for 1 minute. Pour in the white wine and stir to scrape up any browned bits on the bottom of the pan. Add the artichokes and the bouquet garni and bring to a boil. Transfer the pan to the preheated oven and bake for 20 to 30 minutes, or until the artichokes are tender.

✦ Meanwhile in a large ovenproof sauté pan, heat 1 tablespoon of the olive oil over medium-high heat. Sear the veal loin all over for 6 minutes, or until nicely browned. Place the pan in the preheated oven and roast for about 20 minutes for medium-rare. Remove and cover loosely with aluminum foil; let the meat sit for about 10 minutes before slicing.

✦ Remove the vegetables from the oven and discard the bouquet. Stir in the basil.

✦ To serve, spoon a mound of the polenta in the center of each of 2 plates. Slice the veal loin and arrange the slices over the polenta. Spoon some vegetables over the veal and serve at once. *Makes 2 servings*

POLENTA

2½ cups chicken stock or vegetable stock (see Basics) or canned low-salt chicken broth
1 teaspoon salt

½ cup polenta
¼ cup grated Parmesan cheese
2 tablespoons unsalted butter

✦ In a medium saucepan, combine the stock or broth and salt. Bring to a simmer over medium heat. Gradually whisk in the polenta. Reduce heat to low and stir constantly with a wooden spoon for about 20 minutes, or until the polenta is thick and the grains are tender. Stir in the cheese and butter, and serve at once. *Makes 4 servings*

CHOCOLATE-PORT CAKE

Port adds a note of deep, rich flavor to these individual flourless cakes. They are delicious served with Bing cherries or seasonal berries poached in port.

1 cup ruby port wine

⅓ cup corn syrup

2 tablespoons fresh lemon juice

6 ounces bittersweet chocolate, chopped

3½ tablespoons unsalted butter

2 large eggs, separated

½ cup superfine sugar

Pinch of salt

✦ Preheat the oven to 350°F. Butter four 6-ounce ramekins.

✦ In a medium saucepan, bring the port to a boil over high heat and cook to reduce it by half. Add the corn syrup and bring to a boil. Stir in the lemon juice and set aside to cool.

✦ In a small, heavy saucepan over low heat, melt the chocolate with the butter; remove from heat and set aside to cool.

✦ In a medium bowl, using an electric mixer, beat the egg yolks and sugar together until pale and fluffy. Add the chocolate mixture and port syrup and beat until well mixed.

✦ In a separate medium bowl, beat the egg whites and salt until soft peaks form. Gently fold the egg whites into the chocolate mixture. Pour the batter into the prepared ramekins and bake in the preheated oven for 25 minutes, or until a skewer inserted in the center comes out almost clean. *Makes 4 individual cakes*

THE GRILL AT
THE DRISKILL HOTEL

Austin, Texas

In the late 1800s, cattle baron Jesse Lincoln Driskill decided to open a hotel in Austin that would rival the grand establishments of New York, Chicago, and San Francisco. His impressive brick and limestone Romanesque-style show-piece opened in 1896, and it has been a center for social and political life in the Texas state capital ever since.

Jesse Driskill had to sell the hotel when he went bankrupt after a nation-wide drought, followed by a cold spell, killed most of his cattle. However, the Driskill Hotel remained a beloved Austin landmark. Many Texas governors have held their inaugural balls at the hotel, and legend has it that the Texas Rangers met at the Driskill to plan an ambush on Bonnie and Clyde. In 1934, Lyndon Baines Johnson met his future wife Lady Bird at the hotel's restaurant for their first date. Today, the Driskill is a member of Leading Hotels of the World and National Trust Historic Hotels of America.

The grand Driskill lobby has columns, arches, marble flooring, a hand-painted decorative ceiling, and a majestic stained-glass dome. Before dining at the elegant Grill, many people choose to enjoy a drink in the Driskill bar, where antique furniture, intimate seating nooks, and performances on the grand piano by local musicians create a romantic atmosphere. In the dining room, guests are surrounded by luxury, with historic oil portraits, dark wood paneling, etched glass, and a carpet sprinkled with gold Texas stars contributing to the lavish setting.

The Grill's menu features Southwestern flavors such as Green Chili Buttered Quail with Corn and Monterey Jack Fondue (see page 120), imaginative New American cuisine, and impeccably prepared classic dishes. The Grill has received a Mobil Travel Guide four-star award and an AAA's four-diamond award. Executive chef David Bull is known for combining tastes and textures in imaginative and playful ways and was a recipient of *Food & Wine's* magazine's Best New Chef award in 2003. Chef David Bull created the following recipes and presented them to Menus and Music.

Menu

Crabmeat Cocktail with
Watermelon, Mango, and Avocado

~

Green Chili Buttered Quail with
Corn Fondue and Fried Onion Rings

~

Cream of Almond Soup
with Blueberry Cobbler

CRABMEAT COCKTAIL WITH
WATERMELON, MANGO, AND AVOCADO

Horseradish adds zing to this colorful, refreshing first course.

½ cup diced seedless watermelon

½ cup diced mango (see Basics)

½ cup diced avocado

1 teaspoon prepared horseradish

Juice of 1 lime

Salt to taste

8 ounces fresh lump crabmeat, picked
   over for shell

2 watercress sprigs for garnish

✦ In a medium bowl, gently combine the watermelon, mango, and avocado.

✦ In a medium bowl, whisk the horseradish, lime juice, and salt together. Gently stir in the watermelon mixture and crab.

✦ Set a 4-inch ring mold on a salad plate. Gently pack half of the crab cocktail into the mold, reserving any juice. Remove the ring mold and garnish the top with a sprig of watercress. Repeat with the remaining crab cocktail. Alternatively, spoon a mound of crab cocktail in the center of each of 2 plates or into 2 cocktail glasses. Drizzle the reserved juice around each plate or into the cocktail glasses and serve at once. *Makes 2 servings*

*There are four qualities essential to a great jazzman.
They are taste, courage, individuality, and irreverence.
These are the qualities I want to retain in my music.*

—STAN GETZ

Green Chili Buttered Quail with Corn Fondue and Fried Onion Rings

A creamy, spicy-sweet cheese fondue is a perfect foil for richly flavorful quail topped with crisp onions.

Green Chili Butter

½ jalapeño chili*, roasted (see Basics)
½ poblano chili*, roasted (see Basics)
6 tablespoons unsalted butter at room temperature
¼ bunch cilantro
Juice of 1½ limes
Salt to taste

2 partially boned quail or boneless, skinless chicken breasts
Salt and freshly ground pepper to taste

Corn Fondue

2 tablespoons canola oil
Kernels from 1½ ears corn
½ onion, chopped

½ teaspoon ground cumin
¼ cup heavy cream
3 cups shredded Monterey jack cheese
Juice of 1½ limes
Salt to taste

Fried Onion Rings

1 cup all-purpose flour
1 teaspoon paprika
½ teaspoon cayenne pepper
1 teaspoon sugar
1 large onion, thinly sliced and separated into rings
Canola or peanut oil for deep frying
Salt to taste

Fresh cilantro sprigs for garnish

✦ To make the green chili butter: In a food processor or blender, combine all ingredients and purée. Transfer the butter to a bowl large enough to hold the quail or chicken breasts.

✦ To make the quail or chicken: Light a fire in a charcoal grill, or you can use a broiler. Generously sprinkle the quail or chicken with salt and pepper on both sides. Place the quail or chicken in the bowl with the chili butter, coat thoroughly, and set aside for 10 to 15 minutes. Preheat the broiler, if using.

✦ Grill the quail or chicken over hot coals, or under the preheated broiler 2 to 3 inches from the heat source for 2 to 3 minutes on each side, basting with any remaining chili butter before turning to grill, after turning to broil. Remove from heat and let rest for 5 minutes. Cut each quail in half, if using.

✦ To make the fondue: In a medium sauté pan, heat the canola oil over medium heat and sauté the corn, onion, and cumin for 3 minutes; do not let the corn brown. Pour in the cream and bring to a boil.

✦ Transfer the corn mixture to a food processor or blender and purée. Add the cheese and process until smooth. Stir in the lime juice and salt; set aside and keep warm.

✦ To make the fried onion rings: In a pie plate, combine the flour, paprika, cayenne, and sugar. Add the onion rings and toss with the flour mixture until completely coated.

✦ In a Dutch oven or deep fryer, heat 3 inches of the canola or peanut oil until some flour dropped in sizzles. Deep-fry the onion rings in 2 batches until golden brown, about 3 minutes. Using a slotted spoon, transfer the onion rings to paper towels to drain. Sprinkle with salt.

✦ To serve, arrange 2 quail halves or 1 chicken breast on each of 2 warmed plates. Spoon some of the fondue next to the quail or chicken and arrange a few onion rings on top of the quail or chicken. Garnish with cilantro and serve at once.

Makes 2 servings

*Available at many produce stores and supermarkets (see Glossary).

CREAM OF ALMOND SOUP WITH BLUEBERRY COBBLER

Warm golden-crusted blueberry cobblers are surrounded by chilled almond cream. Stunning for dessert and also delicious for breakfast or lunch the next day.

CREAM OF ALMOND SOUP

2 tablespoons cornstarch
1 tablespoon water
¾ cup half-and-half
2 tablespoons slivered almonds, lightly toasted (see Basics)
1½ tablespoons Frangelico or Amaretto liqueur*
2 tablespoons sugar
1 tablespoon almond paste, chopped

COBBLER DOUGH

½ cup all-purpose flour
1 tablespoon sugar
¼ teaspoon salt
4 tablespoons cold unsalted butter, diced
Drops of ice water

BLUEBERRY FILLING

3 cups fresh or frozen blueberries
2 tablespoons all-purpose flour
½ cup plus ½ tablespoon sugar
½ tablespoon unsalted butter, diced
½ teaspoon *each* ground cinnamon and nutmeg
1 teaspoon vanilla extract

4 mint sprigs for garnish

✦ To make the soup: In a small bowl, stir the cornstarch and water together; set aside.

✦ In a medium saucepan, combine the half-and-half, almonds, liqueur, sugar, and almond paste. Bring to a boil over medium heat. Stir in the cornstarch mixture to thicken, and simmer for 5 minutes. Transfer to a food processor or blender and purée. Pour the soup into a bowl and refrigerate for at least 2 hours, or until completely chilled.

✦ Preheat the oven to 375°F. Rub four 3-inch ramekins with butter and spoon in a little sugar to coat the bottom and sides; knock out the excess.

✦ To make the dough: In a medium bowl, combine the flour, sugar, and salt. Add the butter and rub it in with your fingertips until the dough resembles coarse crumbs. Add ice water drop by drop and stir with a fork until the dough just holds together. On a lightly floured surface, form the dough into a ball. Cover in plastic wrap and refrigerate for 30 minutes.

✦ On a lightly floured surface, roll the dough out to a ¼-inch thickness. Using a 3-inch round biscuit cutter or an upended drinking glass, cut out rounds of the dough to cover the tops of the prepared ramekins; set aside.

✦ To make the blueberry filling: In a medium bowl, combine all the ingredients. Gently toss until the blueberries are evenly coated. Place the blueberry mixture in the prepared ramekins and top each with a round of dough. Bake in the preheated oven for 20 minutes, or until the dough is golden brown.

✦ Ladle one-fourth of the soup into each of 4 chilled soup bowls or plates. Unmold a warm blueberry cobbler in the center of each bowl, garnish with a mint sprig, and serve at once. *Makes 4 servings*

*Frangelico is hazelnut liqueur; amaretto is almond liqueur.

THE BISTRO AT
HOTEL MAISON DE VILLE

New Orleans, Louisiana

Resonating with the grace and style of a slower, more pleasure-rich era, Maison de Ville and its Bistro are imbued with the history of the city of New Orleans. Built on the site of a Choctaw Indian portage between Lake Pontchartrain and the Mississippi River, New Orleans was established by the French in 1718 and was then named the capital of the Louisiana Territory. In 1762, at the end of the Seven Years War, France ceded all territory west of the Mississippi River, including New Orleans, to Spain. The city remained under Spanish rule until 1800, when Napoleon forced Spain to return the Louisiana Territory to France. The Creoles were descendents of these early French and Spanish settlers, and they maintained close ties with their European homelands. Interested in the arts and fine cuisine, the Creoles considered themselves paradigms of culture and elegance on the American frontier.

With the Louisiana Purchase in 1803, New Orleans became part of the United States. However, the Creoles tried to live much as they always had and retired behind high walls into their private homes and courtyards. Most new American settlers in New Orleans chose to live across Canal Street in what is now the Central Business District, and those of means developed the Garden District, even further away from the Creole Vieux Carré.

The two-story Hotel Maison de Ville, which means "townhouse" in French, was rebuilt around 1800 after a fire in the French Quarter. Today, the hotel reflects a genteel Southern lifestyle, with its high-ceilinged, antique-filled rooms. The property's seven Audubon Cottages were named for the illustrious painter John James Audubon, who produced a portion of his *Birds of America* series in 1821 while residing in what is now Cottage Number One. The Maison de Ville courtyard has a cast-iron fountain, an original brick patio, and lush semitropical greenery and flowers. This setting was much enjoyed by playwright

125

Tennessee Williams, who often stayed in room No. 9, where he completed *A Streetcar Named Desire* before purchasing his own house in the French Quarter.

The Bistro was opened in 1986, and its red leather banquettes, beveled-glass mirrors, crisp white tablecloths, and cane chairs create a cozy Parisian-style ambiance. Alfresco dining is available in the courtyard, weather permitting. The Bistro has launched the careers of some of New Orleans's best-known chefs and today is a spot favored by other great restaurateurs of the city. Maître d' Patrick Van Hoorebeek has assembled a wine list that is educational for beginners and a treasure trove for experts. The following recipes were created by executive chef Greg Picolo, a Louisiana native who cooks in the Creole style. Picolo's sophisticated menu showcases traditional dishes and innovative seasonal cuisine. Popular with hotel guests and locals alike, The Bistro is a culinary mecca that captures the spirit of New Orleans.

Menu

Smoked Salmon and Endive Rémoulade

~

Broiled Chicken with Pineapple-Avocado Relish
and Deep-Fried Asparagus

~

Coconut Custard with Pecan Crust and
Caramelized Banana-Brandy Sauce

Smoked Salmon and Endive Rémoulade

An easy-to-make first course that can also be made with cooked shrimp in place of the salmon.

RÉMOULADE SAUCE

¼ cup mayonnaise (for homemade see Basics)

½ tablespoon drained capers, chopped

½ teaspoon catsup

¼ teaspoon prepared horseradish

Juice of ½ lemon

Dash of Tabasco, or more to taste

1 teaspoon Worcestershire sauce

½ tablespoon minced fresh flat-leaf parsley

1 large or 2 small endives

4 slices smoked salmon, finely diced

✦ In a medium bowl, stir together all the rémoulade ingredients. Set aside.

✦ Remove 6 outer leaves from the endive(s) and set the leaves aside. Using a sharp knife, thinly slice the remaining endive(s) crosswise. In a large bowl, toss the endive slices with the rémoulade sauce.

✦ Spoon some of the smoked salmon into each of the 6 reserved endive leaves. Arrange 3 filled leaves on each of 2 plates, top with the endive salad, and serve at once. *Makes 2 servings*

The memory of things gone is important to a jazz musician. Things like old folks singing in the moonlight in the back yard on a hot night or something said long ago.

—LOUIS ARMSTRONG

Broiled Chicken with Pineapple-Avocado Relish and Deep-Fried Asparagus

A spectacularly delicious combination of flavors and textures. The bright, lively relish is also delicious with broiled trout fillets.

Pineapple-Avocado Relish

Two 1-inch-thick fresh pineapple
   slices, cored
Salt and freshly ground pepper to taste
½ small tomato, finely diced
½ small red onion, finely diced
1 celery stalk, finely diced
½ teaspoon minced garlic
Juice of ½ lemon
Juice of ½ lime
¼ cup extra-virgin olive oil

¼ teaspoon minced fresh tarragon
1 small avocado, peeled, pitted, and
   diced

2 boneless, skinless chicken breast
   halves
Salt and freshly ground pepper to taste
½ teaspoon minced garlic
Extra-virgin olive oil for coating
Deep-Fried Asparagus (recipe follows)

✦ To make the pineapple-avocado relish: Preheat the broiler. Sprinkle the pineapple slices with salt and pepper. Broil the pineapple 4 inches from the heat source for 3 minutes on each side, or until beginning to char. Let cool and dice.

✦ In a medium bowl, combine the pineapple, tomato, onion, celery, garlic, lemon juice, lime juice, olive oil, tarragon, and salt and pepper to taste. Use now, or cover and refrigerate for up to 1 day. Just before broiling the chicken, gently stir the avocado into the relish and let stand at room temperature.

✦ Preheat the broiler. Rub the chicken generously with olive oil and season with salt, pepper, and garlic. Broil the chicken 6 inches from the heat source for 10 minutes on each side, or until the chicken is opaque throughout and the juices run clear.

✦ To serve, arrange 5 deep-fried asparagus spears in the center of each of 2 plates and top with a chicken breast. Spoon a generous amount of the pineapple-avocado relish over and serve immediately. *Makes 2 servings*

(continued)

Deep-Fried Asparagus

10 asparagus stalks
½ cup all-purpose flour
Salt and freshly ground pepper to taste
½ cup milk

1 egg, beaten
½ cup dried bread crumbs
Canola oil or peanut oil for
   deep-frying

✦ Blanch the asparagus and begin to heat the oil for deep frying before starting the chicken.

✦ In a large pot of salted boiling water, blanch the asparagus for 3 minutes. Drain and run the asparagus under cold water to stop the cooking process; set aside.

✦ In a pie plate, stir the flour, salt, and pepper together. Dredge the asparagus in the flour mixture. In a pie plate, beat the milk and egg together. Coat the asparagus with the egg mixture. Place the bread crumbs in a pie plate and coat the asparagus with the crumbs. Place the asparagus on a plate and refrigerate until chilled, about 20 minutes. This helps the batter to adhere.

✦ In a Dutch oven or deep-fat fryer, heat 3 inches of canola or peanut oil until a bit of batter sizzles when added. Deep-fry half of the asparagus until golden brown, about 2 minutes. Using a slotted spoon, transfer the asparagus to paper towels to drain. Deep-fry the remaining asparagus. *Makes 2 servings*

Coconut Custard with Pecan Crust and Caramelized Banana-Brandy Sauce

A rich, luscious dessert; one fabulous bite will transport you to New Orleans.

Pecan Crust

1 cup finely crushed pecans

1 tablespoon all-purpose flour

½ cup powdered sugar, sifted

2 tablespoons unsalted butter

Coconut Custard

¾ cup heavy cream

¼ cup sweetened shredded coconut

1 egg

1 egg yolk

Caramelized Banana-Brandy Sauce

2 tablespoons unsalted butter

1 small banana, sliced into 1-inch thick slices

1 tablespoon light brown sugar

½ teaspoon vanilla extract

¼ cup brandy

✦ To make the crust: Preheat the oven to 325°F. Butter two 8-ounce ramekins.

✦ In a medium bowl, use a fork to combine the pecans, flour, sugar, and butter until crumbly. Press the dough into the ramekins to coat the bottom and sides and bake in the preheated oven for 5 minutes. Remove from the oven and let cool.

✦ To make the custard: In a heavy saucepan, combine the cream and coconut. Cook over medium-low heat, stirring constantly, for 10 minutes, or until reduced by one-third. Remove from heat and let cool to room temperature.

✦ In a small bowl, whisk the egg and egg yolk together. Fold the egg mixture into the coconut mixture. Spoon the coconut cream into the ramekins. Transfer the ramekins to a baking dish. Fill the dish with water to reach halfway up the sides of the ramekins. Bake in the preheated 325°F oven for 20 minutes, or until a skewer inserted into the center out clean. Let cool to room temperature, for at least 20 minutes before serving. If not serving within 1 hour, refrigerate the custards.

✦ To make the sauce: In a small saucepan, melt the butter over medium-high heat until it foams. Add the banana slices and sauté for 2 minutes, or until browned. Stir in the brown sugar and sauté for 1 minute. Remove from heat and stir in the vanilla and brandy. Pour over the custards and serve at once. *Makes 2 individual custards*

MARCEL'S

Washington, D.C.

Flawless service complements Marcel's Belgian-influenced French cuisine served in an atmosphere of comfortable luxury. Diners enjoy sophisticated classics that owe their strong, robust flavors to chef Robert Wiedmaier's Flemish roots.

Marcel's spacious dining room is decorated in French country style with flowers, iron grillwork, and handsome tapestries. A jazz pianist performs every evening at the lively wine bar, and during summer months a patio offers alfresco dining. For a truly magnificent occasion, an evening at Marcel's can be combined with a concert at Washington's famed Kennedy Center. The restaurant's three-course pre-theater dinner includes free limousine service to and from the Kennedy Center and the option of enjoying coffee and dessert after the performance.

Chef Wiedmaier, who was born in Germany, is of Belgian descent and began his culinary education in the Netherlands. He went on to work at Michelin-starred restaurants in Brussels before moving to Washington, D.C. After cooking at several well-known restaurants in the nation's capital, Wiedmaier opened Marcel's in 1999, naming the restaurant after his eldest son.

Using high-quality fresh ingredients, chef Wiedmaier brings French flavors to the Washington area. To ensure that each meal lives up to his exacting standards, the chef carefully trains each member of his team and meets with the dedicated staff every day. The restaurant's sommelier will suggest wines by the glass to pair with each course or a special bottle from the list of primarily French varietals.

Marcel's consistently receives top Zagat rankings and was the recipient of the Restaurant Association of Metropolitan Washington's Best Fine Dining Award in 2004. The following recipes were created by chef Robert Wiedmaier and presented to Menus and Music.

Menu

Roasted Tomato Soup with
Goat Cheese Flans and Parmesan Crisps

~

Roasted Squab and Celery Root Purée with
Wild Mushrooms and Red Wine Sauce

~

Tower of Chocolate

ROASTED TOMATO SOUP WITH
GOAT CHEESE FLANS AND PARMESAN CRISPS

Roasting tomatoes enhances the flavor of this outstanding soup, which surrounds a creamy goat cheese flan topped with Parmesan and thyme crisps. If you don't have time to make the crisps, serve the soup with crusty bread.

8 tomatoes, halved

3 shallots, minced

1 garlic clove, minced

2 tablespoons minced fresh thyme

4 slices bacon, chopped

2 tablespoons olive oil

2 cups chicken stock or vegetable
   stock (see Basics) or canned low-salt
   chicken broth

2 cups heavy cream or half-and-half

Salt and freshly ground white pepper
   to taste

Goat Cheese Flan (recipe follows)

PARMESAN CRISPS

½ cup grated Parmesan cheese, plus
   2 tablespoons for sprinkling

1 tablespoon minced fresh thyme

½ sheet thawed frozen puff pastry,
   halved crosswise

2 small handfuls microgreens or mixed
   baby salad greens

✦ Preheat the oven to 325°F. Arrange the tomatoes in a baking dish and sprinkle with the shallots, garlic, and thyme. Bake in the preheated oven for 50 to 60 minutes, or until soft and shriveled.

✦ In a large, heavy saucepan, fry the bacon in the olive oil over medium-low heat until crisp. Using a slotted spoon, transfer the bacon to paper towels to drain. Pour off all but 2 tablespoons of the fat. Add the roasted tomatoes, shallot, garlic clove, thyme, and any juice. Pour in the chicken stock or broth and simmer for 20 minutes. Stir in the cream or half-and-half and simmer for 15 minutes.

✦ Transfer the soup to a food processor or blender and purée. Pour through a fine-mesh sieve into a saucepan and season with salt and pepper.

(continued)

✦ To make the crisps: Preheat the oven to 375°F. On a small, rimmed baking sheet, combine the 2 tablespoons Parmesan and the thyme. Stir to blend, then spread evenly. Slice the puff pastry sheet in half lengthwise and generously sprinkle it with the ½ cup Parmesan cheese. Cut the dough into 4 long strips and roll the strips into very thin straws about 10 inches long. Roll the straws in the cheese and thyme mixture until the mixture adheres to the straws. Bake in the preheated oven for 8 to 10 minutes, or until golden brown.

✦ To serve, reheat the soup if necessary. Unmold a goat cheese flan in the center of each of 2 soup bowls. Carefully ladle the tomato soup around each flan. Top each flan with some microgreens, lay 2 Parmesan crisps across, and serve immediately. *Makes 6 to 8 servings*

GOAT CHEESE FLANS

2 eggs

One 4-ounce log fresh white goat
   cheese at room temperature

Salt and freshly ground pepper to taste

✦ Preheat the oven to 300°F. Lightly coat two 4-ounce ramekins with olive oil or butter.

✦ In a medium bowl, beat the eggs, goat cheese, salt, and pepper together until smooth. Pour the cheese mixture into the prepared ramekins and transfer them to a baking dish just large enough to hold them. Fill the dish with hot water halfway up the sides of the ramekins. Bake in the preheated oven for 25 to 30 minutes, or until a skewer inserted in the center comes out almost clean. Remove from the oven and let cool. *Makes 2 flans*

Jazz today, as always in the past, is a matter of thoughtful creation, not mere unaided instinct. —DUKE ELLINGTON

ROASTED SQUAB AND CELERY ROOT PURÉE WITH WILD MUSHROOMS AND RED WINE SAUCE

CELERY ROOT PURÉE
½ tablespoon unsalted butter
½ slice bacon, cut into ¼-inch-wide
  slices
½ small celery root, peeled and diced
½ potato, peeled and diced
½ cup chicken stock (see Basics) or
  canned low-salt chicken broth

Two 1-pound squabs
Salt and freshly ground pepper to taste

2½ tablespoons unsalted butter
½ tablespoon olive oil
2 cups dry red wine
½ cup chicken stock (see Basics) or
  canned low-salt chicken broth
2 tablespoons veal demi-glace*
2 shallots, sliced
8 ounces wild mushrooms, such as
  chanterelles or porcini
2 tablespoons chopped fresh flat-leaf
  parsley

✦ To make the celery root purée: In a medium, heavy saucepan, melt the butter and add the bacon. Cook over medium-low heat for 3 minutes, or until the fat renders. Add the celery root, potato, and ½ cup stock or broth. Cook for 10 minutes, or until the vegetables are soft and the stock or broth evaporates. Transfer the celery root mixture to a food processor or blender and purée; set aside.

✦ Cut the backbones of the squabs so they can be spread flat. Heavily lean on the squabs or hens to crack the breast and rib bones. Be careful not to break through the breast meat and skin. Bone the breasts, but leave the leg bones in and the skin on.

✦ Season the squabs with salt and pepper. In a large sauté pan, melt ½ tablespoon of the butter with the olive oil over medium-high heat. Add the squabs, skin side down, and cook for 10 minutes, or until the skin is a crisp golden brown. Turn over and cook on the other side for 5 minutes for rare; if you press the squabs they should feel like a medium-rare steak or the fleshy part of your thumb. Transfer to a plate and cover loosely with aluminum foil to keep warm.

✦ Place the sauté pan used to cook the squab over medium-high heat and pour in the wine and ½ cup stock or broth. Stir to scrape up any browned bits on the bottom of the pan. Cook until the liquid is reduced by half. Stir in the demi-glace.

✦ In a large sauté pan, melt the remaining 2 tablespoons butter over medium-high heat and sauté the shallots and mushrooms for 5 minutes, or until the mushrooms release their liquid and then become dry. Stir in the parsley and set aside.

✦ To serve, dip a soup spoon into the celery root purée and bring up a rounded spoonful. Invert the bowl of a second soup spoon over the top of the purée and mold into a quenelle shape. Place 2 or 3 quenelles in the center of each of 2 plates. Cut the squabs in half and arrange them on top of the purée. Spoon the sautéed mushrooms around the purée, spoon the red wine sauce over, and serve at once.

Makes 2 servings

*Available at specialty foods stores and some supermarkets (see Resources).

TOWER OF CHOCOLATE

A tall mold of luscious chocolate mousse surrounded by chocolate meringue logs, crème anglaise, and raspberry coulis is a dramatic way to finish a special dinner.

COCOA MERINGUES

2 egg whites at room temperature

Pinch of salt

3 tablespoons granulated sugar

¼ cup plus 1 tablespoon powdered sugar, sifted

1 tablespoon unsweetened cocoa powder

CHOCOLATE MOUSSE

2 tablespoons granulated sugar

3 ounces milk chocolate, preferably Valrhona or Callebaut, chopped

½ cup plus 2 tablespoons heavy cream

½ teaspoon vanilla extract

Raspberry Coulis (see Basics)

Crème Anglaise (see Basics)

Fresh raspberries for garnish

✦ To make the meringues: Preheat the oven to 275°F. Line a baking sheet with buttered parchment paper or a silpat.

✦ In a medium bowl, using an electric mixer, beat the egg whites and salt until soft peaks form. Add the granulated sugar and beat until stiff, glossy peaks form.

✦ In a small bowl, stir together the powdered sugar and cocoa. Gently fold the cocoa mixture into the egg whites.

✦ Fill a pastry bag fitted with a no. 4 tip, or a plastic bag, with the meringue. If using a plastic bag, cut 1 corner diagonally. Pipe the meringue across the length of the prepared baking sheet in 8 straight lines. Bake in the preheated oven for 1 hour.

✦ Let the meringues cool to the touch. Using a serrated knife, slice the meringues into 4-inch and 5-inch lengths. Use now, or store in an airtight container for up to 1 week.

✦ To make the chocolate mousse: Choose two tall, narrow ring molds or glasses or two clean tomato paste cans with both lids removed. Coat with canola oil. Add 1 tablespoon sugar to each mold, and twirl to coat the inside; knock out the excess sugar. Place on a clean plate and set aside.

✦ In a double boiler or stainless-steel bowl over simmering water, melt the chocolate.

✦ In a deep bowl, using an electric mixer, beat the cream on medium speed until it thickens enough to hold a pattern in the center of the bowl but is still loose around the sides.

✦ Fold the cream into the melted chocolate a little at a time and gently stir until smooth. Stir in the vanilla. Spoon the mousse into the prepared molds and refrigerate for 2 to 3 hours before serving.

✦ Unmold a chocolate mousse in the center of each of 2 chilled plates. Arrange half of the meringue logs around the mousse, with the flat sides facing the mousse. Place a few raspberries on top of the chocolate mousse. Spoon raspberry coulis in a circle about 1 inch from each tower. Spoon a circle of crème anglaise inside the circle of raspberry coulis. Garnish each plate with a few raspberries and serve.

Makes 2 servings

MOOSE'S
San Francisco, California

Moose's is a bit of magic. Every evening it becomes a place for special occasion dining, a hangout for movers and shakers, and a sports bar. Everyone in the lively, diverse crowd feels they're at an epicenter of what's happening in San Francisco, and somehow Moose's has once again captured the essence of the city.

After strolling under the neon glow of the giant blue moose outside and making their way past the always-busy bar, diners are seated in a handsome room fronted by large windows that open onto Washington Square, a grassy park anchored by the majestic Saints Peter and Paul church. Moose's grand piano, bustling open kitchen, and stylish patrons make this North Beach neighborhood classic a perfect antidote for foggy San Francisco evenings. It is also a great place to wake up slowly on a weekend morning over a fabulous Sunday brunch.

Ed and Mary Etta Moose, two San Francisco icons, created this gem of a restaurant in a city renowned for fine dining and great jazz spots. Fortunately it's possible to enjoy wonderful New American cuisine here while listening to jazz performed every evening by local musicians. My favorite table for two is just inches away from the grand piano, and most tables in the room are within earshot of the jazz performers. Moose's has been awarded *Wine Spectator* magazine's Award of Excellence for its impressive wine list. Offering over four hundred selections, the list represents nearly all the world's major wine regions, with emphasis on small-scale producers.

The following recipes were created by executive chef Jeffrey Amber, whose acclaimed cooking is creative, precise, and full-flavored. Amber makes use of wild fish and organic produce and meats from local farms and ranches to create California-inspired cuisine for the nightly party that is Moose's.

Menu

Arugula Salad with Oranges,
Goat Cheese, and Toasted Almonds

~

Pan-Roasted Duck Breast with
Garnet Yams and Huckleberry Sauce

~

Poached Lady Apples with
Mascarpone Mousse and Cranberry Coulis

ARUGULA SALAD WITH ORANGES, GOAT CHEESE, AND TOASTED ALMONDS

1 tablespoons sherry vinegar

3 tablespoons extra-virgin olive oil

Splash of fresh orange juice

½ shallot, minced

4 or 5 fresh chives, minced

Salt and freshly ground pepper to taste

4 handfuls baby arugula leaves

½ seedless navel orange, peeled and segmented (see Basics)

2 tablespoons fresh white goat cheese, crumbled

2 tablespoons slivered almonds, toasted (see Basics)

Aged balsamic vinegar for garnish (optional)

✦ In a small bowl, whisk the vinegar, olive oil, orange juice, shallot, chives, salt, and pepper together; set the vinaigrette aside.

✦ In a large bowl, gently toss the arugula, orange segments, and goat cheese with the vinaigrette. Season with salt and pepper to taste and toss again.

✦ Arrange a mound of salad on each of 2 plates and sprinkle with the toasted almonds. If desired, drizzle with balsamic vinegar. *Makes 2 servings*

It bugs me when people try to analyze jazz as an intellectual theorem. It's not. It's feeling. —BILL EVANS

Pan-Roasted Duck Breast with Garnet Yams and Huckleberry Sauce

Richly flavorful duck is complemented by a fruity sauce. If huckleberries are unavailable, make the sauce with blueberries or cherries.

2 boneless duck breast halves, with skin
Salt and freshly ground pepper to taste
Leaves from ½ bunch thyme, minced

Huckleberry Sauce
1 shallot, thinly sliced
½ cup ruby port
1 cup veal demi-glace*, chicken stock
  (see Basics), or canned low-salt
  chicken broth

½ cup fresh or frozen huckleberries or
  blueberries
Salt and freshly ground pepper to taste

2 garnet yams, peeled
1 cup fresh orange juice
Salt to taste
2 tablespoons olive oil

✦ Using a sharp knife, score a crisscross pattern in the skin of the duck breasts, and sprinkle with salt and pepper. Layer half of the thyme in the bottom of a small baking dish. Top with the duck breasts and cover the duck with the remaining thyme. Cover and refrigerate for at least 6 hours. Before cooking, let the duck sit at room temperature for about 15 minutes.

✦ To make the berry sauce: In a medium saucepan, combine the shallots and port. Cook over medium heat to reduce to 1 or 2 tablespoons. Add the demi-glace, stock or broth, and berries and simmer over low heat for 20 minutes. Transfer to a food processor and purée. Strain the sauce through a fine-mesh sieve into the same saucepan, season with salt and pepper, and keep warm.

✦ Put the yams in a medium saucepan and add water to cover by 1 inch. Pour in the orange juice and season generously with salt. Cook over medium-high heat for 25 minutes, or until the yams are easily pierced with a knife; do not overcook. Drain and let cool. Slice the yams crosswise into 1-inch thick rounds and set aside.

✦ In a large sauté pan, heat 1 tablespoon of the olive oil over medium-high heat. Lower heat to medium and cook the duck breasts, skin side down, for 7 to 10 minutes, or until crisp and golden brown. Pour off the fat. Turn the breasts over and cook for 3 to 4 minutes for medium-rare, or until rosy pink in the center. Transfer to a cutting board, skin side up, and loosely cover with aluminum foil.

✦ In a large sauté pan, heat the remaining 1 tablespoon olive oil over medium-high heat and sauté the yams for 2 minutes on each side, or until golden. Transfer to a plate and season with salt and pepper.

✦ Arrange the yams on each of 2 plates. Place the duck breasts skin side down and cut into thin lengthwise slices. Fan each breast out in front of the yams, spoon the sauce over the duck, and serve at once. *Makes 2 servings*

*Available at specialty foods stores and some supermarkets (see Resources).

POACHED LADY APPLES WITH
MASCARPONE MOUSSE AND CRANBERRY COULIS

The combination of tiny sweet-tart lady apples, creamy mascarpone, and tangy cranberry coulis makes a luscious dessert.

CRANBERRY COULIS
½ cup fresh or frozen cranberries, or
   ¼ cup dried cranberries
¼ cup fresh orange juice
1 teaspoon fresh lime juice
1 sprig fresh mint
Salt and freshly ground pepper to taste

1 cup dry red wine
4 lady apples, or other small apples,
   peeled and tossed in lemon juice
½ cup (4 ounces) mascarpone cheese*
   at room temperature
4 tablespoons sugar

✦ To make the cranberry coulis: If using dried cranberries, soak them in hot water to cover for 30 minutes; drain.

✦ In a small saucepan, combine the cranberries, orange juice, lime juice, and mint. Cook over medium-low heat until the liquid reduces by half. Transfer to a food processor or blender and purée. Strain through fine-mesh sieve into the same saucepan and season with salt and pepper. Remove from heat and set aside.

✦ In a small bowl, whisk the mascarpone and 2 tablespoons of the sugar together until the sugar dissolves. Cover and refrigerate for at least 30 minutes.

✦ In a medium saucepan, combine the red wine and the remaining 2 tablespoons sugar. Bring to a boil over high heat. Add the apples, reduce heat to medium-low, and cook for about 8 minutes, or until a knife easily pierces the apples. Drain and let cool.

✦ Spoon half of the mascarpone mousse onto each of 2 plates. Top with an apple and spoon some cranberry coulis over the apples. *Makes 2 servings*

*Available at many grocery stores and most Italian foods stores (see Glossary).

NORTH POND

Chicago, IL

Nestled within Chicago's beloved Lincoln Park is a ten-acre pond that is North Pond restaurant's namesake. Years ago, the pond was a favorite ice-skating location, and in 1912 an Arts and Crafts–style structure was built on its bank as a warming room and changing area for skaters. Although North Pond is no longer used for ice skating, the charming Arts and Crafts building now houses one of Chicago's finest restaurants.

Diners can feast on chef Bruce Sherman's brilliant cooking while enjoying views of the Chicago skyline and Lincoln Park. One airy dining room is surrounded on three sides by tall glass French doors, and in the main room a large Illinois fieldstone fireplace, decorative period pieces, and copper-accented oak bar create a warm, intimate space.

Proponents of the Arts and Crafts movement believed in simple design and good craftsmanship created by human beings rather than by machines. In part a reaction to the Industrial Revolution, the movement was popular around the 1900s and its principles are still relevant for chef Bruce Sherman today. Sherman, one of *Food & Wine* magazine's Best New Chefs of 2003, describes his food as "reflective of the ingredients themselves." Using seasonal products from small local organic farms, he is dedicated to building relationships among growers, chefs, and North Pond patrons. The restaurant adds one dollar to the price of each bottle of wine on its list and matches the amount with an additional dollar. This money goes to organizations that support sustainable agriculture, local farmers, and diverse food choices around the world.

Sherman, who studied at the École Supérieure de Cuisine Française in Paris and worked at several Michelin-starred restaurants in France, showcases traditional European flavors and French-based culinary techniques. His cooking is characterized by subtlety, restraint, and impeccable technique. The restaurant's food-friendly wine list focuses primarily on small American producers.

To reach North Pond restaurant, diners follow a path through Lincoln Park to reach a lovely oasis of culinary magic tucked away within urban Chicago. The following recipes were created by chef Bruce Sherman and presented to Menus and Music.

Menu

Potato Waffles with Poached Eggs, Smoked Salmon, and Lemon-Caviar Butter

~

Thyme-Basted Rib-eye Steak, Carrots, Quinoa, and Red Wine Butter Sauce

~

Vanilla Wafers with Hazelnut Mousse and Espresso Caramel

POTATO WAFFLES WITH POACHED EGGS,
SMOKED SALMON, AND LEMON-CAVIAR BUTTER

Sophisticated comfort food. This stunning starter is also delicious for breakfast or brunch, and best made with farm fresh eggs and hardwood smoked salmon.

POTATO WAFFLES

1 egg

1 egg yolk

1 cup crème fraîche* (for homemade
  see Basics) or heavy cream

Freshly grated nutmeg and ground
  white pepper to taste

1 pound russet potatoes, peeled

½ teaspoon salt

LEMON-CAVIAR BUTTER

1 teaspoon water

1 teaspoon fresh lemon juice

5 tablespoons cold unsalted butter,
  cubed

Salt to taste

1 tablespoon American-farmed
  sturgeon caviar

3 cups water

2 tablespoons distilled white vinegar

2 eggs

4 slices cold-smoked salmon

1 teaspoon American-farmed sturgeon
  caviar for garnish

Fresh herb sprigs, watercress, or
  micro-greens for garnish

✦ Preheat the waffle iron. In a large bowl, whisk the egg, egg yolk, crème fraîche or heavy cream, nutmeg, and white pepper together.

✦ Using the coarse holes of a box grater, shred the potatoes onto a dish towel. Enclose the shredded potato in the towel and wring both ends of the towel to remove as much moisture from the potato as possible. Add the potato and salt to the egg mixture and stir until blended.

✦ If the waffle iron isn't nonstick, lightly brush it with butter. Evenly spread the potato mixture onto the hot waffle iron, close the lid, and cook for 5 to 6 minutes, or until the waffles are evenly browned and the potatoes are cooked through.

(continued)

✦ Meanwhile, make the lemon-caviar butter: In a small saucepan, bring the water and lemon juice to a simmer over medium heat. Whisk in the butter, piece by piece, until the mixture thickens slightly. Remove from heat and stir in the salt. Cover and set aside.

✦ In a small saucepan, bring the water and vinegar to a boil. Reduce heat to low and bring the water to a bare simmer. Crack each egg into a saucer, slip the eggs into the simmering water, and cook for 3 minutes. While the eggs cook, stir the caviar into the reserved lemon butter.

✦ Remove the waffle from the iron and cut it in half diagonally. Arrange a waffle half on each of 2 plates. Rest a second waffle half on top, placing it at an angle. Arrange a slice of smoked salmon over the center of each waffle.

✦ Using a slotted spoon, lift out the poached eggs, tamping any excess moisture with a towel, and carefully place 1 egg atop the salmon on the bottom waffle. Spoon the lemon-caviar butter over the eggs and top each egg with a dollop of caviar. Garnish with herbs, watercress, or micro-greens and serve at once.

Makes 2 servings

*Available at specialty foods stores and many supermarkets (see Glossary).

Thyme-Basted Rib-eye Steak, Carrots, Quinoa, and Red Wine Butter Sauce

Photographed for the cover of this book, this dish involves quite a bit of preparation, but it is especially delicious and rewarding to make for celebratory occasions. You can start the red wine sauce the day before.

Red Wine Butter Sauce
1 teaspoon olive oil
1 shallot, thinly sliced
½ celery stalk, chopped
½ carrot, peeled and chopped
1 cup dry red wine
1 garlic clove, crushed
2 sprigs fresh thyme
1¼ cups chicken stock (see Basics) or canned low-salt chicken broth
4 tablespoons cold unsalted butter, chopped
Salt and freshly ground pepper to taste

Quinoa
1 cup quinoa*
1 slice bacon, chopped
1 shallot, minced
2 cups chicken stock (see Basics) or canned low-salt chicken broth

1 tablespoon each minced fresh chives and flat-leaf parsley
Salt and freshly ground pepper to taste

One 16-ounce thick-cut (2 inches) rib-eye steak with bone
2 tablespoons salt
1 tablespoon freshly cracked black pepper
¼ cup cold unsalted butter, chopped
5 sprigs fresh thyme
3 unpeeled garlic cloves

Roasted Carrots
1 tablespoon olive oil
3 carrots, peeled and cut ½ inch thick on the diagonal
1 garlic clove, crushed
1 teaspoon minced fresh flat-leaf parsley
Salt and freshly ground pepper to taste

✦ To make the red wine sauce: In a small saucepan, heat the olive oil over medium heat and sauté the shallot, celery, and carrot for 2 minutes, or until softened. Add the wine, garlic, and thyme and boil for 15 minutes, or until the liquid evaporates and becomes a glaze. Add the chicken stock or broth and boil until only a syrupy liquid remains. Pour the syrup through a fine-mesh sieve into a small saucepan; use a rubber spatula to clean out the pan and to press the solids through the sieve. Use the syrup now as the base for the sauce, or cover with plastic wrap and refrigerate for up to 1 day.

✦ To make the quinoa: Put the quinoa in a fine-mesh sieve and rinse with cold water until the water runs clear. In a medium saucepan, fry the bacon for 3 minutes over medium heat, or until the fat renders. Add the shallot and sauté for 2 minutes; do not brown. Add the quinoa and chicken stock or broth, raise heat to medium-high, and bring to a boil. Cover, reduce heat to low, and simmer for 17 minutes. Remove from heat and stir in the chives and parsley. Season with salt and pepper; set aside.

✦ To prepare the steak: Preheat the oven to 400°F. Heat a cast-iron or other heavy ovenproof frying pan over medium-high heat. Season both sides of the steak with salt and pepper. Swirl the butter into the hot pan and add the meat. Top the steak with half the thyme sprigs and garlic and add the remaining thyme and garlic to the pan. Cook for 5 to 6 minutes, or until the meat forms a crust on the bottom. Baste the meat regularly, carefully spooning the pan liquid over the herbs atop the meat. Turn the meat over and continue basting 5 to 7 minutes for medium-rare. Transfer the meat to a plate and let rest for about 10 minutes.

✦ Meanwhile, make the carrots: In a large frying pan, heat the olive oil over medium-high heat for 1 minute. Add the carrots and garlic and cook for 3 minutes without shaking the pan. Turn the carrots over and cook undisturbed for 3 minutes, or until tender and lightly browned. Remove from heat and stir in the parsley, salt, and pepper.

✦ To serve, place the frying pan with the steak in the preheated oven for 3 to 4 minutes to warm the meat. Heat the red wine syrup until it just starts to simmer. Remove from heat and whisk in the butter, piece by piece, until incorporated; season with salt and pepper.

✦ Lightly press the quinoa into two 3-inch ramekins and unmold onto each of 2 plates, or place a scoop of quinoa on each of 2 plates. Spoon the carrots next to the quinoa and pool some of the red wine butter sauce in front. Slice the steak against the grain into long slices and arrange the slices over the sauce. Grind some pepper over the steak, garnish with parsley or thyme, if desired, and serve at once.

Makes 2 servings

*Available at many supermarkets and specialty foods stores (see Glossary and Resources).

Vanilla Wafers with Hazelnut Mousse and Espresso Caramel

Vanilla Wafers

5 tablespoons unsalted butter at room
   temperature
¾ cup powdered sugar
2 egg whites
½ teaspoon vanilla extract
⅓ cup all-purpose flour

Hazelnut Mousse

½ cup milk
4 tablespoons sugar
1 egg yolk
¼ teaspoon vanilla extract

½ tablespoon unflavored gelatin
3 tablespoons Nutella
¼ cup heavy cream

Espresso Caramel

½ cup sugar
¼ cup water
¼ cup heavy cream, heated
1½ teaspoons instant espresso powder
1½ teaspoons unsalted butter at room
   temperature
½ teaspoon salt

✦ To make the vanilla wafers: Preheat the oven to 450°F. Line a baking sheet with parchment paper or a silpat or spray it lightly with nonstick cooking spray.

✦ In a large bowl, using an electric mixer, cream the butter and sugar together until light and fluffy. Mix in the egg whites and vanilla. Add the flour and mix to make a smooth batter.

✦ Spoon teaspoonfuls of the batter onto the prepared baking sheet. Flatten with the back of a spoon to make thin, 2-inch rounds. Bake in the preheated oven for 3 minutes, or until golden brown around the edges. Remove from the oven and let the cookies cool on the pan.

✦ To make the hazelnut mousse: In a small saucepan, combine the milk and 2 tablespoons of the sugar. Cook over medium heat until bubbles form around the edges of the pan.

There is no such thing as a wrong note. —Art Tatum

✦ In a medium bowl, whisk the egg yolk and the remaining 2 tablespoons sugar together until pale. Gradually whisk a thin stream of the hot milk mixture into the egg yolk mixture; then whisk until all of the milk is incorporated. Return to the small saucepan. Cook over low heat, stirring constantly, for 3 to 5 minutes, or until the mixture thickens enough to coat the back of the spoon. Remove from heat, stir in the vanilla, and let cool for 2 or 3 minutes. Stir the gelatin into the still-warm custard until dissolved. Strain through a fine-mesh sieve into a medium bowl. Whisk in the Nutella until smooth; set aside and let cool.

✦ In a medium bowl, using an electric mixer, beat the cream until stiff peaks form. Stir one-third of the whipped cream into the mousse mixture. Gently fold in the remaining whipped cream and refrigerate for at least 1 hour or up to 24 hours.

✦ To make the caramel: In a small saucepan, combine the sugar and water and cook over medium heat until a rich caramel color. Remove from heat and carefully whisk in the hot cream and instant coffee. Let cool to warm, then whisk in the butter and salt. Add warm water as needed to achieve the desired consistency.

✦ To serve, place a single wafer in the center of each of 2 plates. Using an ice cream scoop or a tablespoon, scoop a serving of the mousse on top of the wafer. Place a second wafer on top of the mousse. Spoon some of the caramel around the perimeter of the plate, drizzle caramel over the top cookie, and serve at once.

Makes 4 servings

TABLA
New York, New York

Opened in 1998, Tabla serves chef Floyd Cardoz's fabulous New American cuisine spiced with the sensual flavors of India. With views of Madison Square Park and the Flatiron Building, the restaurant offers two different dining experiences. In the formal second-story main dining room, Cardoz uses classic cooking techniques to create refined dishes that are infused with Indian spices, and at the informal Bread Bar downstairs, his Indian home-style dishes and street snacks are made from seasonal local ingredients.

Danny Meyer is one of the masterminds behind Tabla, and the restaurant is part of his Union Square Hospitality Group (USHG), which also includes highly acclaimed Union Square Cafe, Gramercy Tavern, and Eleven Madison Park. Meyer is a jazz lover who also runs Blue Smoke and the Jazz Standard, where guests can enjoy great jazz in New York City while feasting on food from Blue Smoke upstairs.

Chef Cardoz was born in Bombay, raised in Goa, and trained in India, Switzerland, and New York. For years, he searched for an original way to showcase the aromatic flavors of his homeland. Cardoz spent five years at the renowned Lespinasse restaurant in New York City and was executive sous-chef under Gray Kunz, who he considers his mentor. "When I arrived at Lespinasse, there were only four Indian spices in the cabinet," he recalls. "When I left, we had incorporated over twenty-five." Cardoz hopes that everyone in American will soon be using Indian spices. "They should be as common as soy sauce and ketchup," he says.

Tabla's balcony-level dining room is reached by climbing a wide staircase past a Robert Kushner mosaic on the wall of the staircase landing. The elegant room is buzzing with energy and filled with vibrant paintings, curved walls in shades of red and green, and exotic dark woods. Here, chef Cardoz creates dazzling dishes that draw inspiration from India's twenty-eight states. Tabla's gracious staff is always knowledgeable about the cuisine. Every evening before the restaurant opens, the chefs and staff have a meeting so that servers can get detailed explanations about the menu.

The Bread Bar downstairs has small tables, a dozen chairs at the bar, and a breezy, shaded patio out front for more casual dining. The decor even includes two tablas (small Indian drums) hung over the espresso machine. Indian breads such as roti, naan, and paratha emerge from three tandoori ovens and reinventions of Goan foods are served family style.

The following recipes were created by chef Floyd Cardoz and dedicated to Kenny Barron, the renowned jazz pianist and avid cook, who considers Tabla one of his favorite restaurants. It seems fitting that Kenny Barron, who has created a musical identity all his own, should admire the cooking of Floyd Cardoz, who has forged his own culinary identity.

Menu

Goan-Style Mussels with Calamari

~

Seared Striped Bass with Eggplant, Shiitakes, Green Mango, and Tamarind Gastrique

~

Spiced Pumpkin Cake with Cranberry-Orange Compote

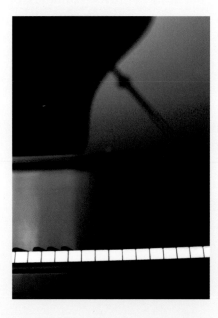

GOAN-STYLE MUSSELS WITH CALAMARI

Piquant and fiery, these mussels are served in a style traditional to Goa, a state on the west coast of India famous for its seaside resorts.

1½ tablespoons canola oil
½ teaspoon brown mustard seeds*
1 sprig fresh curry leaves*
1 small onion, quartered and sliced
1 teaspoon minced fresh ginger
1 tablespoon tamarind paste*
½ Thai chili*, thinly sliced
1 large garlic clove, minced
Salt and freshly ground pepper to taste

20 black mussels, scrubbed and
  debearded
8 ounces squid, cleaned and sliced into
  rings, with some tentacles
1½ tablespoons fresh cilantro leaves,
  minced
Indian flat bread such as naan, or
  crusty French bread for serving

✦ Heat a large sauté pan over medium-high heat. Swirl in the canola oil and heat until almost smoking. Add the mustard seeds and cook until they begin to pop. Add the curry leaves and onion and sauté for 5 minutes, or until the onion is golden brown. Add the ginger, tamarind, chili, and garlic and sauté for 5 minutes. Season with salt and pepper.

✦ Add the mussels and cover the pan with a lid. Cook until all the mussels have opened, about 5 minutes; discard any that do not open. Add the squid and cilantro and cook for 2 minutes, or until the squid is opaque. Serve immediately, with Indian flat bread or French bread. *Makes 2 servings*

*Available at Indian and Asian markets and specialty foods stores (see Glossary and Resources).

SEARED STRIPED BASS WITH EGGPLANT, SHIITAKES, GREEN MANGO, AND TAMARIND GASTRIQUE

Tangy, earthy, and sweet flavors combine in this outstanding dish.

TAMARIND GASTRIQUE

2 ounces (¼ cup) jaggery* or packed
  brown sugar
1 tablespoon cold water, plus 1 cup
  warm water
½ cup tamarind paste*
¼ cup chicken stock (see Basics) or
  canned low-salt chicken broth
2 tablespoons coriander seeds*, toasted
  (see Basics) and crushed
1½ teaspoons Szechwan peppercorns*,
  toasted (see Basics) and crushed
1½-inch piece fresh ginger, peeled and
  minced
Salt to taste

1 Japanese eggplant, quartered
  lengthwise and cut into 1-inch-thick
  crosswise slices
2 tablespoons canola oil
5 shiitake mushrooms, stemmed and
  quartered
½ teaspoon brown mustard seeds*
½ tablespoon unsalted butter
1 shallot, minced
½ teaspoon minced ginger
1 small garlic clove, minced
1 large slice peeled green mango* or
  green apple, finely diced
Salt and freshly ground pepper to taste
½ tablespoon minced fresh chives
Flour for dredging
2 striped bass fillets

✦ To make the gastrique: In a medium saucepan, combine the jaggery or brown sugar and the 1 tablespoon water. Bring to a boil over medium heat and cook until the sugar dissolves.

✦ In a small bowl, combine the tamarind paste and the 1 cup warm water. Soak the pulp for 5 to 10 minutes, or until soft. Using your fingers, rub the pulp until it dissolves and the seeds are free of pulp. Strain and discard the seeds and fibers. Add the tamarind and stock or broth to the sugar mixture and cook until the mixture is smooth. Add the coriander seeds, peppercorns, ginger, salt, and pepper and simmer until the mixture reduces to a jelly. Strain the gastrique though a fine-mesh sieve into a bowl and set aside.

(continued)

✦ In a large pot of boiling salted water, blanch the eggplant for 3 minutes; drain and set aside.

✦ In a large sauté pan, heat 1 tablespoon of the canola oil over medium-high heat and sauté the mushrooms until they release their liquid and become dark brown. Add the mustard seeds and cook until the seeds pop. Reduce heat to medium-low and stir in the butter, shallot, ginger, and garlic; cook for 3 minutes. Add the eggplant, green mango or apple, and salt. Remove from heat and stir in the chives. Set aside and keep warm.

✦ In a large frying pan, heat the remaining 1 tablespoon canola oil over medium heat. Season the fish fillets with salt and pepper and lightly dredge them in flour. Fry the fish, skin side down, for 3 minutes, or until golden brown on the bottom. Turn the fish over and cook for 2 minutes, or until opaque throughout.

✦ Spoon the eggplant-shiitake mixture onto each of 2 plates and place a striped bass fillet over the vegetables. Spoon the tamarind gastrique around the plate and serve at once. *Makes 2 servings*

*Available at Indian and Asian markets and specialty foods stores (see Glossary and Resources).

Music is your own experience, your thoughts, your wisdom. If you don't live it, it won't come out of your horn.

—CHARLIE PARKER

Spiced Pumpkin Cake with Cranberry-Orange Compote

6 tablespoons unsalted butter

¼ cup cream cheese at room
   temperature

¾ cup sugar

½ cup pumpkin purée

1 egg

¼ teaspoon *each* cinnamon and ginger

⅛ teaspoon *each* nutmeg and
   vanilla extract

¾ cup all-purpose flour

½ teaspoon baking powder

Pinch of salt

Cranberry-Orange Compote
   (recipe follows)

✦ Preheat the oven to 325°F. Butter or oil four 6-ounce ramekins.

✦ In a large bowl, cream the butter, cream cheese, and sugar together.

✦ In a medium bowl, combine the pumpkin purée, egg, cinnamon, ginger, nutmeg, and vanilla. Stir to blend. Add the pumpkin mixture to the butter mixture and stir until well combined.

✦ In a small bowl, stir the flour, baking powder and salt with a whisk. Stir the flour mixture into the pumpkin mixture until just combined. Spoon the batter into the prepared ramekins and bake in the preheated oven for 18 minutes, or until a skewer inserted in the center comes out clean. Let the cakes cool for 10 minutes. Unmold each cake onto a dessert plate and serve with a spoonful of cranberry-orange compote. *Makes 4 individual cakes*

Cranberry-Orange Compote

⅓ cup sugar

¼ cup water

1 strip orange zest (see Basics)

2 tablespoons fresh orange juice

¾ cups (3 ounces) fresh or frozen
   cranberries

✦ In a medium saucepan, combine the sugar, water, orange zest, and orange juice. Bring to a boil over medium-high heat and cook until the sugar dissolves. Add the cranberries and simmer until they pop, 5 to 10 minutes. Remove from heat and let cool. *Makes about 1 cup*

VETRI

Philadelphia, Pennsylvania

Vetri's superb full-flavored Italian cuisine proves over and over again that a great dining experience is a cause for celebration. Vetri is housed in the same small townhouse where Le Bec-Fin, one of the finest restaurants in Philadelphia history, first opened its door. Today, the restaurant's tiny dining room boasts warm yellow walls with hand-painted murals, dark wood wainscoting, wide-plank flooring, and soft lighting provided by Italian frosted-glass sconces. On a wooden sideboard in the center of the room sits chef Marc Vetri's pride and joy: an antique meat slicer, circa 1936. Every plate of antipasto ordered at the restaurant is garnished with meltingly thin, delicate slices of prosciutto carefully cut by chef Vetri himself.

A Philadelphia native, Marc Vetri started cooking to support himself while studying his first love, jazz guitar. Vetri soon realized that he belonged in the kitchen, and apprenticed himself to Wolfgang Puck at Granita in Los Angeles. His culinary education continued in Italy, where he learned to butcher, make wine, press olive oil, and prepare prosciutto. Eventually, the young chef moved back to his hometown to open the restaurant of his dreams. Along with re-creating the classic dishes he had loved in Italy, Vetri has created the kind of restaurant where each diner knows that the chef is personally cooking their meal. In 1999, Marc Vetri was a recipient of *Food & Wine* magazine's Best New Chefs award.

Inspired by the freshest possible ingredients, the menu showcases the vibrant flavors of rustic Italian cuisine and the feather-light pasta for which chef Vetri is renowned. The restaurant has won *Wine Spectator* Award of Excellence, and co-owners Vetri and Jeffrey Benjamin consider wine an integral part of the Vetri experience. Especially popular are the five- and seven-course tasting menus, with each dish accompanied by a carefully chosen glass of wine. The following recipes were created by chef Marc Vetri and presented to Menus and Music.

Menu

Tri-Color Beet Salad with
Goat Cheese and Walnuts

~

Lamb Loins with Fava Bean Purée

~

Saffron Risotto with Charred Scallions

~

Strawberries Marinated in Balsamic Syrup
with Crème Fraîche

TRI-COLOR BEET SALAD WITH GOAT CHEESE AND WALNUTS

A superb salad of perfectly balanced tastes, colors, and textures.

1 red beet

1 yellow beet

2 small Chioggia beets

2 cups kosher salt (optional)

Juice of ½ lemon

2 tablespoons extra-virgin olive oil

Salt and freshly ground pepper to taste

1 cup mixed baby salad greens

2 tablespoon chopped walnuts

¼ cup crumbled fresh white goat cheese

✦ Preheat the oven to 400°F. Trim the beet stems to 1 inch.

✦ Put the beets in a baking dish just large enough to hold them and cover them with the salt. Alternatively, wrap each beat in aluminum foil and arrange in a baking dish. Bake in the preheated oven for 1 hour, or until the beets can be pierced all the way through with a knife. Remove from heat, let cool, trim, and peel.

✦ Cut the beets into different shapes such as batons, cubes, and rounds and transfer them to a medium bowl. Add the lemon juice, olive oil, salt, and pepper and toss until the beets are thoroughly coated. Using a slotted spoon, transfer the beets to the center of each of 2 plates, reserving the vinaigrette.

✦ Add the salad greens to the reserved vinaigrette and toss to coat the greens. Surround the beets with the salad greens and sprinkle over the walnuts and goat cheese. *Makes 2 servings*

I've found you've got to look back at the old things and see them in a new light.

—JOHN COLTRANE

LAMB LOINS WITH FAVA BEAN PURÉE

A simply elegant dish to serve in late spring and early summer when fava beans are in season. At other times of the year, chef Marc Vetri makes a delicious purée using cooked cannellini beans in place of the fava beans.

FAVA BEAN PURÉE

2 pounds fava beans, shelled
   (about 2 cups)
2 tablespoons olive oil
½ onion, coarsely chopped
½ cup chicken stock, canned low-salt
   chicken broth, or water
1 teaspoon sherry vinegar
Salt and freshly ground pepper to taste

2 lamb loins, noisettes, or eye of the
   rack, about 8 ounces each
Salt and freshly ground pepper to taste
1 tablespoon olive oil
1 tablespoon unsalted butter
Extra-virgin olive oil and coarse salt
   for garnish

✦ In a pot of salted boiling water, blanch the fava beans for 1 minute. Drain and run under cold water. Using your fingernails, pinch off a small piece of the skin and slip each bean out.

✦ In medium sauté pan, heat 1 tablespoon of the olive oil over medium-low heat and sauté the onion for 3 minutes, or until translucent. Pour in the chicken stock, broth, or water and bring to a boil. Reduce heat to low, add the fava beans, and simmer for 5 minutes. Remove from heat and transfer the bean mixture to a food processor. Add the vinegar, the remaining 1 tablespoon olive oil, and the salt and pepper and purée.

✦ Preheat the oven to 400°F. Season the lamb with salt and pepper. Heat a large, heavy frying pan over medium-high heat and swirl in the olive oil and butter. When the oil starts to smoke, add the lamb and cook until browned. Turn and cook until browned on the other side. Transfer the pan with the lamb to the preheated oven and bake for 3 to 4 minutes for rare, or 5 to 6 minutes for medium-rare. Remove from the oven and let the meat rest for 6 to 7 minutes.

✦ Spoon a pool of fava bean purée onto each of 2 plates. Slice the lamb into disks and arrange on top of the purée. If desired, garnish with a drizzle of olive oil and a sprinkling of coarse salt and serve at once. *Makes 2 servings*

Saffron Risotto with Charred Scallions

3 cups water, chicken stock (see Basics), or canned low-salt chicken broth

2 tablespoons olive oil, plus more for coating

1 small onion, finely diced

½ cup Canaroli or Arborio rice

½ cup dry white wine

Generous pinch of saffron threads

6 scallions, washed and well dried

1 tablespoon unsalted butter

¼ cup grated Parmesan cheese

Salt and freshly ground pepper to taste

✦ In a medium saucepan, bring the water, stock, or broth to a simmer. Maintain at a low simmer over low heat.

✦ In a large sauté pan, heat the 2 tablespoons olive oil over medium heat and sauté the onion for 3 minutes, or until translucent. Add the rice and stir for 3 to 4 minutes, or until opaque. Pour in the wine and stir until the wine is completely absorbed. Add the saffron and ½ cup of the water, stock, or broth. Stir constantly until the liquid is absorbed. Repeat, adding liquid ½ cup at a time, until the rice is al dente, about 20 minutes.

✦ In the meantime, heat a grill pan, iron skillet, or heavy sauté pan over high heat. Coat the scallions with olive oil and char them in the pan until they are soft and almost burnt, about 10 minutes; set aside.

✦ Remove the risotto from heat and stir in the butter, Parmesan cheese, salt, and pepper. Spoon the risotto into the center of each of 2 plates, top with 3 charred scallions, and serve at once. *Makes 2 servings*

Strawberries Marinated in Balsamic Syrup with Crème Fraîche

A simple fruit dessert with several intriguing layers of flavor.

¼ cup sugar

¼ cup water

1 tablespoon aged balsamic vinegar

1 pint fresh strawberries, hulled and halved

¼ cup crème fraîche* (for homemade see Basics)

✦ In a small saucepan, cook the sugar over medium heat until it begins to caramelize, about 5 minutes. Carefully add the water and vinegar (they will bubble vigorously) and simmer for 5 minutes. Remove from heat and let cool to room temperature.

✦ Put the strawberries in a medium bowl, and pour the cooled syrup over them. Let stand for at least 1 hour, or up to 6 hours. Spoon the strawberries and syrup into each of 2 bowls and top with a dollop of crème fraîche. *Makes 2 servings*

*Available at specialty foods stores and many supermarkets (see Glossary).

WILD GINGER
Seattle, Washington

After years of traveling and researching traditional Asian cooking, Rick and Ann Yoder conceived the founding principles of Wild Ginger. They wanted to create food that was cooked to order from fresh, quality ingredients and served with grace in a casual atmosphere. The Yoders' deceptively simple concept involves a complex mixture of Asian cooking with Western-style service. Since 1989, they have been fulfilling their dream with panache at their exciting restaurant and satay bar. At the same time, the husband and wife team have created one of Seattle's most popular eating places.

In 2001, Wild Ginger moved from its original location to a renovated historic building in the heart of downtown Seattle. The room's high ceiling, Asian art, and walls of windows create a stunning interior space. An elegant spiral stairway leads up to a small candlelit lounge and private banquet rooms.

The centerpiece of Wild Ginger is the curved satay bar, where juicy lamb, scallops, and marinated boar are grilled, skewered, and served on platters for sharing family-style. Sitting on comfortable stools around the large grill, patrons can sip local brews and watch the cooks grilling, or they can choose to dine at well-spaced tables in the large, airy dining room. The restaurant's seafood and vegetarian dishes are outstanding, as are the Cantonese, Vietnamese, Thai, and Korean plates. Wild Ginger is the perfect place for a late-night meal after a concert at Benaroya Hall, which is just across the street and home to the Seattle Symphony.

Located beneath Wild Ginger is Triple Door, a beautifully restored hall for jazz, blues, cabaret, Latin, and world music. Originally a roaring-twenties era vaudeville club, it has been transformed by Rick and Ann Yoder into a music space with a world-class sound system, luxurious booths, and superb food and libations. The following recipes were created by chef Rick Yoder and presented to Menus and Music.

Menu

Kabocha Squash and Sweet Potato Stew

~

Lemongrass Chicken Satay

~

Halibut with Black Bean Sauce

~

Mango and Sticky Rice with Warm Coconut Sauce

KABOCHA SQUASH AND SWEET POTATO STEW

Thick and comforting, this stew has a sensational combination of flavors and textures. The dish can also be made using acorn squash or other favorite winter squash.

1½ dried bean curd sheets*
½ cup dried tapioca shreds* or small
   pearl tapioca
1½ cups (2½ ounces) rice stick
   noodles*, broken into 1-inch lengths
2½ cups canned coconut milk*
2½ cups water
1 red Thai* or serrano chili, minced
2 tablespoons sugar

Salt to taste
½ small kabocha squash*, seeded,
   peeled, and cut into bite-sized pieces
8 ounces sweet potato or garnet yam,
   peeled, and cut into bite-sized pieces
8 ounces zucchini, cut into bite-sized
   pieces
Fresh cilantro leaves for garnish

✦ Put the dried bean curd sheets in a large bowl and add water to cover. Let stand for 1 hour. Drain and coarsely chop the sheets into 1-inch squares. Put the tapioca in a medium bowl and add hot water to cover. Let stand for 30 minutes. Put the rice noodles in a medium bowl. Add warm water to cover and let stand for 30 minutes.

✦ In a large saucepan, combine the coconut milk, water, chili, sugar, rice noodles, bean curd, tapioca shreds or pearl tapioca, and salt. Bring to a simmer over medium heat. Add the squash, sweet potato or yam, and zucchini and cook for 30 minutes, or until the vegetables are soft but not falling apart. Stir occasionally and do not let the stew boil.

✦ Just before serving, taste and adjust the seasoning. Ladle the stew into bowls and garnish with cilantro leaves. *Makes 6 to 8 servings*

*Available at Asian markets and specialty foods stores (see Glossary and Resources).

*In my music, I'm trying to play the truth of what I am.
The reason it's difficult is because I'm changing all the time.*

—CHARLES MINGUS

LEMONGRASS CHICKEN SATAY

Start marinating the chicken the night before you plan to serve this flavorful, grilled appetizer.

4 boneless, skinless chicken thighs, or
  2 boneless, skinless chicken breast
  halves

MARINADE
1 stalk lemongrass*, white part only,
  peeled and cut into thin crosswise
  slices
2 tablespoons minced fresh ginger
3 garlic cloves, minced

2 tablespoons honey
½ tablespoon Asian sesame oil
½ teaspoon fish sauce*
½ teaspoon Chinese five-spice
  powder*
Salt and freshly ground pepper
  to taste

Green leaf lettuce for garnish
  (optional)

✦ Ask your butcher to pound the chicken flat, or pound it yourself. Put the chicken on a cutting board and use a meat pounder or rolling pin to flatten it to about ¼ inch thick.

✦ In a medium nonreactive bowl, combine all the marinade ingredients and stir to blend. Set aside.

✦ Cut the flattened chicken into strips 2½ inches wide and 6½ inches long. Add the chicken to the marinade and toss to coat. Cover with plastic wrap and refrigerate overnight.

✦ Light a fire in a charcoal grill. Soak 8 to 10 wooden skewers in cold water for 30 minutes. Alternatively, heat a grill pan over medium-high heat.

✦ Skewer the chicken by holding each slice in your hand and carefully threading the skewer lengthwise through the meat.

✦ Place the skewers on the grill or in the grill pan at an angle and grill for 3 minutes, or until they lift off the grill easily. Using tongs, turn the skewers and cook for 3 minutes, or until the chicken is opaque throughout.

✦ Line a serving plate with lettuce leaves, if desired. Arrange the skewers on the plate and serve at once. *Makes 8 to 10 skewers*

*Available at Asian markets and specialty foods stores (see Glossary and Resources).

Halibut with Black Bean Sauce

2 Pacific halibut fillets, or other mild
  white fish
8 paper-thin slices peeled fresh ginger

2 tablespoons Shaoxing wine*
  (Chinese rice wine), or dry sherry
Black Bean Sauce (recipe follows)

✦ Put the halibut in a glass pie plate and cover the fish with the ginger slices. Pour
over the rice wine or sherry. Place the plate in a large steaming basket. Add 3 cups
water to just below the steaming basket in a large saucepan. Bring the water to a
boil, and add the steaming basket to the steamer. Cover and steam the halibut
for 8 minutes, or until a toothpick goes through it easily. Remove from heat and
transfer the fish to a platter; reserve any liquid from the plate for the black bean
sauce. Discard the ginger slices. Cover loosely to keep warm. *Makes 2 servings*

Black Bean Sauce

2 tablespoons coarsely chopped
  unrinsed fermented black beans*
2 tablespoons Shaoxing wine*
  (Chinese rice wine), or dry sherry
½ teaspoon Asian sesame oil
1 tablespoon peanut oil or canola oil
4 garlic cloves, minced
1 teaspoon minced fresh ginger
1 or 2 Thai chilies* minced

Reserved liquid from steamed fish,
  above (optional)
2 teaspoons fish sauce*
½ teaspoon sugar
2 teaspoons cornstarch dissolved in
  1 tablespoon chicken stock
2 scallions, white part only, julienned
2 sprigs fresh cilantro

✦ In a bowl, combine the fermented beans, rice wine or sherry, and sesame oil.
✦ Heat a wok or large, heavy saucepan over medium-high heat. Swirl in the peanut
or canola oil and heat until a piece of garlic sizzles. Stir in the garlic, ginger, and
chili and cook for 1 minute, or until the garlic is golden. Add the fermented bean
mixture, optional reserved liquid, fish sauce, and the sugar. If necessary, add a few
tablespoons more chicken stock or water. Stir until fragrant, then stir in the
cornstarch mixture to thicken.
✦ Arrange the fish on a platter and ladle the sauce over. Garnish with scallions and
cilantro and serve at once. *Serves 2 as a main dish or 4 as part of a larger meal*

MANGO AND STICKY RICE WITH WARM COCONUT SAUCE

Warm, cool, and sweet all at the same time, this dessert is based on a traditional dish of Southeast Asia. Start soaking the sticky rice the day before you plan to serve the dessert.

STICKY RICE
1 cup sticky rice*
½ teaspoon salt
⅓ cup canned coconut milk*

1 large ripe mango
Coconut Sauce (recipe follows)

✦ To make the sticky rice: Put the rice in a fine-mesh sieve and rinse with water until the water runs clear. Transfer the rice to a medium bowl and add water to cover. Refrigerate overnight.

✦ Line a steamer basket with banana leaves or cheesecloth. Drain the rice and distribute it evenly over the leaves or cloth. Cook over boiling water in a covered steamer until tender but not mushy, about 45 minutes. The rice will be sticky. Transfer the rice to a large bowl and stir in the salt and coconut milk.

✦ Hold the mango upright on a cutting board with a narrow side facing you. Using a large knife, cut off one "face" (the flat side) of the fruit. Repeat on the other flat side. Peel the mango and slice at an angle. Fan out the slices on 2 plates. Place a scoop of sticky rice on each plate and top with warm coconut sauce.
Makes 2 servings

COCONUT SAUCE

¼ cup packed palm sugar* or dark
  brown sugar

1 can (13.5 ounces) coconut milk*
½ teaspoon salt

✦ In a small saucepan, combine all the ingredients. Stir to blend. Cook over medium heat for 20 to 30 minutes, or until thickened. Remove from the heat and keep warm. *Makes about ¾ cup*

*Available at Asian and Indian markets and some specialty foods stores (see Glossary and Resources).

YOSHI'S
Oakland, California

Apopular Japanese restaurant and at the same time one of the finest places to hear jazz in the United States, Yoshi's is the creation of Yoshi Akiba, a brilliant and talented San Francisco Bay Area woman. Starting as a simple restaurant in Berkeley and then moving to larger venues because of its increasingly popular mix of sushi and jazz, Yoshi's has entertained Bay Area patrons since 1973.

In 1997, the restaurant and jazz house moved to a fabulously remodeled space in Oakland's historic Jack London Square. Every evening, Yoshi's lounge pulses with energy as patrons converse over glasses of wine, sake, or beer before dinner. The menu highlights artfully arranged sushi, grilled seafood, classic Japanese dishes such as tempura (see page 190) and ohitashi (see page 192), and vegetarian fare. Diners can choose to enjoy traditional Japanese tatami mat seating or dine at tables in a light, airy space filled with natural maple wood, bamboo, and Japanese art. At the sushi bar, expert chefs create sushi and sashimi to order.

In the jazz house adjoining Yoshi's restaurant, it's possible to hear legends at their zenith and young musicians on their way up. McCoy Tyner, Herbie Hancock, Kenny Barron, Ron Carter, James Moody, Bobby Hutcherson and hundreds of other jazz masters have performed here, as have Stefon Harris, Gonzalo Rubalcabo, Kenny Garrett, and other rising stars. The club's programming is unparalleled for its breadth and quality, and live music is performed here 363 days a year. "It's the nicest club in the United States," says jazz singer Nancy Wilson.

From the front row to the back, there's not a bad seat in the house. State-of-the-art sound and lighting, immaculate sightlines, and elegant Japanese design mix with cocktail tables, cozy booths, and large black-and-white photographs of musicians to create an inviting atmosphere for all ages. Yoshi's is committed to encouraging younger audiences to enjoy the experience of a jazz show, and there is a Sunday matinee series with specially priced tickets for families. While listening to jazz, patrons can enjoy delicious sushi, appetizers, salads, and desserts.

Yoshi's has been the center for great jazz and sushi in the Bay Area for more than twenty-five years, and as a dinner spot with music it is unsurpassed.

MENU

MAGURO TUNA SALAD

~

PRAWN AND VEGETABLE TEMPURA

~

OHITASHI

~

GREEN TEA ICE CREAM

MAGURO TUNA SALAD

A sensational salad of mixed greens topped with seared fresh tuna slices and soy-wasabi dressing.

VINAIGRETTE

3 tablespoons rice wine vinegar*

3 tablespoons extra-virgin olive oil

½ teaspoon wasabi powder*

½ teaspoon fresh lemon juice

1 teaspoon minced shallot

Salt and freshly ground pepper to taste

1 tablespoon canola oil

One 5-inch-square block sushi-grade
   tuna fillet

4 large handfuls mixed baby salad
   greens

SOY-WASABI DRESSING

1 tablespoon wasabi powder* mixed
   with ¼ cup water

2 tablespoons soy sauce

1 tablespoon minced shallot

½ teaspoon rice wine vinegar*

Pinch of minced garlic

Toasted sesame seeds for sprinkling
   (see Basics)

✦ In a small bowl, whisk together all the vinaigrette ingredients. Set aside to allow the flavors to blend.

✦ In a large frying pan, heat the canola oil over medium-high heat until almost smoking. Lightly sear the tuna on all sides until opaque; the interior will be rare. Using a sharp knife, cut the tuna into ¼-inch-thick slices.

✦ To make the soy-wasabi dressing: In a small bowl, stir all the ingredients together until just combined. Set aside for 5 minutes to allow the flavors to marry.

✦ In a medium bowl, toss together the salad greens and vinaigrette. Arrange a mound of salad in the center of each of 2 plates and top with the seared tuna slices in a circular pattern. Dot the rare center of each tuna slice with soy-wasabi dressing, sprinkle the salad with sesame seeds, and serve immediately. *Makes 2 servings*

*Available at Asian markets, specialty foods stores, and some supermarkets (see Glossary and Resources).

PRAWN AND VEGETABLE TEMPURA

An assortment of crisp batter-fried prawns and vegetables. Sliced eggplant, asparagus tips, and snow peas may also be used.

4 or 5 prawns or jumbo shrimp, shelled and deveined, tails intact

1 small sweet potato, peeled and cut into thin rounds

1 carrot, peeled and cut into thin 3-inch sticks

2 zucchini, cut into thin 3-inch sticks

4 shiitake or white mushrooms, stemmed

4 green beans

TEMPURA BATTER

1 cup all-purpose flour

1 small egg, beaten

¾ cup ice water

DIPPING SAUCE

¼ cup *each* soy sauce and water

¼ cup mirin* or medium sherry

¼ cup bonito flakes*

✦ Using a sharp knife, cut crosswise incisions in the under section of each shrimp. Turn over the shrimp and make incisions across the back. Rinse lightly and pat dry with paper towels. Pressing down with the thumbs of both hands on the rounded topside of the shrimp, gently straighten out and stretch the shrimp. Place the shrimp and vegetables on a plate.

✦ Line a plate with paper towels. In a deep fryer or Dutch oven, heat 3 inches canola oil over medium-high heat to 365°F.

✦ To make the tempura batter: In a medium bowl, beat the egg and water together. Add the flour all at once and stir to make a lumpy batter.

✦ Drop a bit of batter into the oil. When the batter sinks halfway and then quickly rises to the top, the oil is the right temperature.

✦ Dip each shrimp up to the tail in the batter and slip it into the hot oil. When the shrimp come to the surface, turn and cook the second side. Using tongs or a slotted spoon, transfer the shrimp to paper towels to drain. Dip each vegetable into the batter, shaking off any excess, and deep-fry until the batter is a light beige.

✦ Meanwhile, in a small bowl, stir all the dipping sauce ingredients together.

✦ Arrange the tempura decoratively on each of 2 warmed plates. Serve immediately, with the dipping sauce. *Makes 2 servings*

*Available at Asian markets, specialty foods stores, and some supermarkets (see Glossary and Resources).

OHITASHI

A traditional Japanese dish of boiled spinach with soy-sesame sauce.

OHITASHI SAUCE
1 tablespoon white sesame seeds,
   toasted (see Basics)
2 tablespoons soy sauce
1 tablespoon water

1 teaspoon sugar
1 tablespoon rice wine vinegar*

2 bunches fresh young spinach,
   stemmed and washed

✦ To make the ohitashi sauce: In a small bowl, whisk the sesame seeds, soy sauce, water, sugar, and vinegar together.

✦ Fill a large bowl with ice water. Bring a large pot of water to a boil. Holding the tops of the spinach leaves, dunk the stem end of the leaves into the boiling water for 20 seconds to soften them. Drop the leaves into the boiling water and cook for 10 seconds. Using a slotted spoon, immediately transfer the spinach to the prepared bowl of ice-water to stop the cooking process. Drain. Place the spinach on a cotton kitchen towel and tightly squeeze to remove the moisture. Using your hands, form the leaves into a long, fat roll.

✦ Lay the spinach roll onto a bamboo mat and shape it into a 1-inch- to 1¼-inch-diameter roll by rolling the mat over the spinach. Cut the roll into 1-inch-thick crosswise sections. Arrange the slices on a small plate and pour the ohitashi sauce over. Let stand for 5 to 10 minutes before serving. *Makes 2 servings*

*Available at Asian markets, specialty foods stores, and some supermarkets (see Glossary and Resources).

Rather than simply say, I play jazz, I say I play music.

—KENNY GARRETT

GREEN TEA ICE CREAM

At Yoshi's, scoops of green tea ice cream are served with sweet azuki beans. A simple green tea ice cream can be made by mixing 2 tablespoons powdered green tea, or matcha, with 1 pint of softened vanilla ice cream.

2 egg yolks
1 cup milk
¼ cup sugar
1 cup heavy cream

2 tablespoons powdered green tea
  (matcha)*
⅓ cup hot water

✦ In a medium saucepan, whisk the egg yolks until they are pale. Add the milk and sugar and stir until well mixed. Cook the egg mixture over low heat, stirring constantly, until it thickens enough to coat the back of the spoon. Remove from heat and let cool.

✦ In a small bowl, stir the green tea powder and hot water together. Pour the green tea mixture and cream into the egg mixture and stir until combined. Let cool. Refrigerate the custard for 2 hours. Freeze in an ice cream maker according to the manufacturer's instructions. *Makes 1 pint*

*Available at Asian markets and some specialty food stores (see Glossary and Resources).

BASICS

Artichoke Hearts

Trim off the stems of the artichokes and any dark green leaves. With a large, sharp knife, cut off the top 1 inch of the artichokes. Place the artichokes, stem side down, into a large nonreactive pot in which they fit snugly. Add water to cover the artichokes and bring the water to a boil. Reduce heat and simmer, uncovered, for 30 to 45 minutes, or until a leaf can be easily removed and the artichoke bottoms are tender when pierced with a knife. Using a slotted spoon, transfer the artichokes to a plate and set them aside, upside down, to cool. Using a sharp knife, remove the leaves. Using a teaspoon, dig out the chokes.

Boiled White Rice

2½ cups water   1 cup long-grain rice

In a heavy saucepan, bring the water to a boil. Add the rice, reduce heat to low, cover, and simmer for 20 minutes. Remove from heat and let stand, covered, for 5 to 10 minutes. Fluff with a fork. *Makes 3 cups*

To Peel Chestnuts

Bring a large pot of water to boil. Using a chef's knife, cut off the pointed tips of the chestnuts, then cut a small X in the flat side of each shell. Place the chestnuts in the boiling water and cook for 5 minutes. With a slotted spoon, remove a few chestnuts at a time from the water and peel off the hard shell and thin brown skin. Chestnuts are easier to peel when hot, so leave the nuts in the hot water until you peel them. If the shells and skin are still too hard to peel, boil the chestnuts for 1 more minute.

To Roast Chilies

Roast whole chilies on a grill, directly over the flame on a gas stove, or in a cast-iron frying pan over medium-high heat, turning to char on all sides. Or, cut large chilies into fourths, seed, press to flatten, and char under a preheated broiler. Using tongs, transfer the chilies to a paper or plastic bag, close it, and let the chilies cool for 10 to 15 minutes. Remove from the bag, peel off the skin with your fingers or a small, sharp knife, and core and seed the chilies if charred whole.

To Peel and Segment Citrus Fruit

Cut off the top and bottom of an orange, grapefruit, or lemon down to the flesh, then stand the fruit upright and cut off the peel in sections down to the flesh. Working over a bowl to catch the juice, hold the fruit in one hand and cut between the membranes. Rotate the fruit and let the sections fall into the bowl. Pick out any seeds.

Crème Anglaise

3 egg yolks

⅔ cup sugar

1½ cups milk

1 tablespoon vanilla extract

In a medium bowl, whisk the egg yolks and sugar together until pale and thick enough to form a ribbon on the surface when the whisk is lifted. In a small saucepan, heat the milk over medium-low heat until bubbles form around the edges of the pan. Gradually whisk the hot milk into the egg mixture. Return to the saucepan and cook, stirring constantly, over medium heat until thick enough to coat the spoon. Do not let the mixture simmer or the yolks will scramble. Remove from heat and stir in the vanilla; let cool. Store, covered, in the refrigerator for 3 or 4 days. *Makes about 2 cups*

Crème Fraîche

Mix 2 cups heavy cream with 2 tablespoons buttermilk in a medium bowl. Cover with plastic wrap and let stand at room temperature overnight or until fairly thick. Refrigerate for at least 4 hours. The cream can be stored, covered, in the refrigerator for 3 days. *Makes 2 cups*

To Zest Lemons and Oranges

To make strips: Using a vegetable peeler or sharp paring knife, cut thin strips of the colored part (the zest) of the lemon or orange peel; don't include the white pith underneath, which is apt to be bitter. To grate: Use a grater or zester to remove the zest of the lemon or orange.

Dicing a Mango

Hold the mango upright on a cutting board with a narrow side facing you. Using a large knife, cut off one "face" (the flat side) of the fruit. Repeat on the other flat side. Score the flesh of each half into squares and push each half inside out so it looks like a hedgehog. Cut off each square.

Mayonnaise

1 egg
1 teaspoon Dijon mustard
½ teaspoon salt

1 tablespoon fresh lemon juice
1 cup extra-virgin olive oil

In a blender or food processor, blend the egg, mustard, and salt for 30 seconds. Add the lemon juice and blend for 10 seconds. With the machine running, slowly add the olive oil in a very thin stream until emulsified. Taste and adjust the seasoning. *Makes about 1¼ cups*

Raspberry Coulis

1 pint (2 cups) fresh or
   thawed frozen raspberries
2 tablespoons sugar

Fresh lemon juice or orange juice
   to taste
Grated lemon or orange zest to taste

In a food processor or blender, purée the raspberries. Add the sugar, lemon or orange juice, and zest and purée. Strain through a fine-mesh sieve. Cover and refrigerate until ready to use. *Makes about 1½ cups*

Simple Syrup

In a small, heavy saucepan, combine 1 cup sugar and ⅓ cup water. Bring to a simmer over medium heat. Cook until the sugar has dissolved. Remove from heat and let cool. Pour into an airtight container. Cover and store in the refrigerator for up to 6 months. *Makes about 1 cup*

Toasting Nuts and Seeds

Preheat the ovem to 350°F. Spread the nuts or seeds on a baking sheet and bake, stirring once or twice, for 5 to 10 minutes, or until fragrant and very lightly browned.

Toasting Szechwan Peppercorns

Heat a wok or heavy skillet over medium heat and add the peppercorns in a single layer. Toast, stirring occasionally, for 3 minutes, or until fragrant. Remove and cool before grinding.

To Peel and Seed Tomatoes

Cut out the cores of the tomatoes and cut an X in the opposite end. Drop the tomatoes into a pot of rapidly boiling water for 10 seconds, or until the skin by the X peels away slightly. Drain and run cold water over the tomatoes; the skin should slip off easily. To seed, cut the tomatoes in half crosswise, hold each half upside down over the sink (or a fine-mesh sieve over a bowl, if you want to save the juice), and gently squeeze and shake to remove the seeds.

STOCKS

Beef Stock

4 pounds meaty beef bones, sliced
2 tablespoons olive oil
½ cup dry white wine
1 onion, chopped
1 bay leaf

3 sprigs fresh flat-leaf parsley
6 black peppercorns
3 quarts water
½ cup tomato purée
Salt and freshly ground pepper to taste

✦ Preheat the oven to 400°F. In a roasting pan, toss the bones with the olive oil to coat evenly. Roast for 40 minutes, or until well browned, turning occasionally. Transfer to a stockpot.

✦ Pour the fat out of the roasting pan. Place the pan over medium heat, add the wine, and stir to scrape up the browned bits from the bottom of the pan. Pour this liquid into the stockpot. Add all the remaining ingredients. Bring to a boil and skim off any foam that rises to the top. Simmer slowly, uncovered, for 3 to 4 hours, or until the stock is well flavored.

✦ Strain through a fine-mesh sieve into a bowl and let cool. Cover and refrigerate overnight. Remove and discard the congealed fat on the surface. Store in the refrigerator for up to 3 days. To keep longer, bring to a boil every 3 days or freeze for up to 3 months. *Makes about 4 cups*

Chicken Stock

2 onions, coarsely chopped

Bouquet garni: 4 parsley sprigs,
  4 peppercorns, 1 thyme sprig, and
  1 bay leaf, tied in a cheesecloth
  square

4 pounds chicken bones and bony parts
  such as backs, necks, and wings

2 carrots, peeled and chopped

3 celery stalks, chopped

5 garlic cloves

✦ In a stockpot, combine all the ingredients and add water to cover by 2 inches. Bring to a boil and skim off any foam that forms on the surface. Reduce heat to low and simmer, uncovered, for 1½ to 2 hours, or until the stock is well flavored. Strain through a fine-mesh sieve and let cool completely. Cover and refrigerate overnight. Remove and discard any congealed fat on the surface. Store in the refrigerator for up to 3 days. To keep longer, bring to a boil every 3 days, or freeze for up to 3 months. *Makes about 6 cups*

Vegetable Stock

1 cup coarsely chopped carrot

1 cup chopped celery

2 unpeeled onions, quartered, or 2
  leeks, washed and chopped

2 cups vegetable scraps and trimmings

2 or 3 fresh parsley sprigs

1 or 2 bay leaves

½ teaspoon minced fresh thyme

½ teaspoon ground pepper

8 cups water, or more as needed

✦ In a large stockpot, combine all the ingredients and bring to a boil. Reduce heat to low and simmer for 1 to 2 hours. Remove from heat and strain through a fine-mesh sieve.

✦ Cover and refrigerate for up to 3 days. To keep longer, bring the stock to a boil every 3 days, or freeze for up to 3 months. *Makes about 8 cups*

GLOSSARY

ANDOUILLE SAUSAGE: Smoky, spicy, and sweet, this delectable coarse-grained pork sausage is commonly used in Creole and Cajun cooking.

BONITO FLAKES: Savory, salty flakes of dried and very finely shaved bonito fish (a type of tuna) that create a strong, clean fish flavor. Bonito flakes are primarily used to make dashi, a Japanese cooking stock.

BROWN MUSTARD SEEDS: Commonly used in Indian cuisine, brown mustard seeds have a warm, nutty flavor when toasted in oil and release a sharp, pungent aroma when crushed. They are also used to make traditional French mustards.

CARDAMOM: This intensely flavorful spice is made from cardamom seeds, which grow in pods. It can be purchased ground, as seeds, or still in the pod. Black cardamom is a common spice in Indian cuisine. In some parts of the Middle East, green cardamom is used to flavor coffee, and white cardamom (made by bleaching green cardamom) is a traditional baking spice in northern Europe.

COCONUT MILK: A creamy white liquid made by steeping shredded fresh or unsweetened dried coconut meat in boiling water; canned coconut milk is also available. Don't confuse coconut milk with the clear liquid found inside a fresh coconut, or with sweetened coconut cream.

CORIANDER SEEDS: An essential ingredient in curry powder, coriander seeds have a distinctive lemony aroma and flavor and combine well with ginger. They are used in North African, Asian, and Latin American cuisine. Fresh coriander leaves are called cilantro or Chinese parsley.

CHILIES

JALAPEÑO: These hot green or red chilies are about 2 inches long and have a thick, juicy flesh.

POBLANO: A somewhat mild black-green chili with a thick skin, usually about 4 inches long and 2½ inches wide. When dried, the poblano is known as an ancho or mulato chili.

SERRANO: Slender green and red chilies that are about 1½ inches long and ½ inch wide. They are similar to the jalapeño but slightly hotter.

THAI/BIRD: Hotter than jalapeño or serrano chilies, these tiny, aromatic red or green chilies can be used both fresh and dried. Birds enjoy the wild varieties because they do not respond to spiciness as humans do.

CRÈME FRAÎCHE: A tangy thickened cream that is a staple in most French kitchens. Slightly milder than sour cream, crème fraîche can be whipped like heavy cream and will not separate when heated. To make your own, see Basics.

CURRY LEAVES: Fresh curry leaves have a light, delicate flavor and are harvested from the curry tree. They quickly lose their flavor when dried and are not an ingredient of the dried spice mix known as curry powder. Commonly used in Sri Lankan and South Indian cuisine, curry leaves can be refrigerated for a few days, or frozen.

DRIED BEAN CURD SHEETS/TOFU SKINS: Made by lifting off the skin formed on soy milk after it has been heated and then cooled, bean curd sheets are high in protein. Also called bean curd skins or yuba, the sheets should be softened in warm water before being used as wrappers or added to soups and stews.

EASTER EGG RADISHES: Mild-flavored globe radishes that come in a variety of beautiful colors such as rose pink, white, and purple.

FENNEL POLLEN: With an amazing taste somewhere between fennel seed, anise, and curry, aromatic fennel pollen is harvested from the tiny yellow flowers of the fennel plant. Prized in Italy and also harvested in California, fennel pollen can be used to flavor everything from desserts to fish, pork, and steamed vegetables.

FERMENTED BLACK BEANS: Fermented soybeans preserved in salt are a Chinese cooking staple. Pungent and salty, they are usually sold in plastic bags and will keep indefinitely in a cool, dark place.

FILÉ POWDER: Also known as gumbo filé, this powder is made from the ground dried leaves of the sassafras tree. First used by the Choctaw Indians from the Louisiana bayou country, it is an important ingredient in Cajun and Creole cooking. The powder has a woody flavor reminiscent of root beer and is used as a thickening agent.

CHINESE FIVE-SPICE POWDER: A popular blend of spices that has been used in China since ancient times. Spicy and sweet, the powder typically consists of ground star anise, Szechwan peppercorns, cloves, fennel seeds, and cinnamon.

FISH SAUCE: A salty staple of southeast Asian kitchens, this clear reddish-brown liquid is made from salted, fermented fish, usually anchovies.

GREEN MANGOES: Mangos can be enjoyed at every stage of ripeness. The unripe fruit, with a white flesh and green skin, has a tart refreshing taste that is similar to that of green apples.

JAGGERY: An unrefined light brown sugar made from the sap of palm trees or sugarcane juice. Jaggery, also known as gur, has a sweet, winey taste and is used primarily in India.

KABOCHA SQUASH: A dark green winter squash with an orange flesh. Sometimes called Japanese squash or Japanese pumpkin, kabochas usually weigh about 3 pounds and can be cooked like acorn squash.

LEMONGRASS: Resembling a large woody scallion, fresh lemongrass stalks provide a subtle citrus flavor that is used extensively in Asian cuisine. If possible, use fresh lemongrass, as much flavor is lost in the drying process. Choose pale green moist stalks and discard the tough outer leaves.

Cut off the upper leaves at the point where they branch out from the white bulb, smash the bulb to release the juice, and chop or slice crosswise into thin disks. Like bay leaves, lemongrass is often used to flavor a dish, and then removed before serving. Store fresh lemongrass stalks in the refrigerator, wrapped in moist paper towels.

MASCARPONE: A delicately flavored triple-cream fresh cheese from Lombardy. It is sold in plastic containers in specialty foods stores and some supermarkets.

MATCHA/GREEN TEA POWDER: Matcha, literally "powdered tea," is made of high-grade Japanese green tea leaves. It has a distinctive mellow flavor that is slightly sweet. The bright jade green super-fine powder has been used for centuries in the traditional Japanese tea ceremony, where it is whisked with hot water to make a frothy tea.

MIRIN: Mirin is a low-alcohol sweet, golden Japanese rice wine. It adds a subtle sweetness and flavor to many Japanese dishes and is tradisionally used in making sauces and glazes.

POMEGRANATE MOLASSES: A thick, dark syrup made from reduced pomegranate juice. Pomegranate molasses has a rich, tart flavor and is a traditional ingredient in Middle Eastern cuisine.

QUESO FRESCO: Commonly used in Latin American cooking, fine-grained queso fresco is a mild, crumbly cheese that does not melt.

QUINOA: Quinoa (pronounced "keen-wa"), is a grain that contains eight essential amino acids and is therefore a complete protein. It cooks in only 10 to 15 minutes. Prized by the ancient Incas and Aztecs, quinoa is technically a seed and is a staple of South American cuisine.

RAMPS: A type of wild onion with a garlicky, peppery flavor. Ramps are a springtime delicacy in Appalachia as well as in the Great Lakes region, where they are known as wild leeks. Choose ramps that have 2 or 3 bright green leaves and a small white bulb attached to a purplish stem. To use, remove the papery outer leaf, cut off any roots, and wash carefully.

Rice Stick Noodles: Made from rice flour, these mildly flavored dried noodles come in many widths. The noodles should not be cooked to soften: instead, soak them in warm water until soft.

Rice Wine Vinegar: With a delicate, clean taste, unseasoned Japanese rice wine vinegar has a flavor that is milder and less acidic than most vinegars made from grapes.

Sambal Oelek: This hot chili paste is commonly used in Southeast Asia and China. The spicy condiment is typically made from dried chilies, salt, and vinegar. Stored in the refrigerator, it will keep indefinitely.

Shaoxing Wine/Chinese Rice Wine: A mellow, amber-colored rice wine used for cooking and drinking that is brewed in the city of Shaoxing in China's Zhejiang province. This good-quality rice wine is aged from eighteen months to one hundred years and has a flavor similar to dry sherry.

Shiso: Also called Japanese basil, or perilla, fragrant shiso leaves make a lovely garnish and are traditionally used in making sushi. A member of the same family as basil and mint, the plant has broad triangular leaves with jagged edges.

Szechwan Peppercorns: Used frequently in Szechuan and Hunanese cooking and an essential component of Chinese five-spice powder, Szechwan peppercorns are the dried berry of a type of ash tree and not actually a member of the pepper family. They have a subtle woody flavor and are slightly numbing to the tongue.

Sticky Rice: Not to be confused with short-, medium-, or long-grain rice, this rice is commonly used in Southeast Asia, where its stickiness is preferred in such dishes as Mango and Sticky Rice with Coconut Sauce (see page 185). The rice must be rinsed and soaked before steaming.

Tapioca Shreds: Also called tapioca sticks, these short crinkle-shaped strips of dried tapioca are most commonly used in Vietnamese cooking.

Tamarind Paste and Tamarind Concentrate: The fruit of a tropical tree, tamarind is an ingredient in Indian chutneys and sauces as well as Worcestershire sauce. Tamarind adds sourness, with more depth than lemon juice. Tamarind pods contain small seeds and a sticky pulp that, when dried, becomes extremely sour. The paste is made from shelled, seeded, and partially dried tamarind pulp. To use, soak the paste in water, then push it through a sieve to remove the fibers and any seeds. Tamarind concentrate is made from tamarind pulp.

Wasabi: Sold as a paste or powder, wasabi is a hot, sharp Japanese horseradish, a little spicier than white horseradish. To use the light green powder, mix it with an equal amount of water to make a paste.

Resources for Cooks

The CMC Company
P.O. Box 322
Avalon, NJ 08202
800-262-2780
www.thecmccompany.com
Hard-to-find ingredients from around the world, including Szechwan peppercorns, five-spice powder, Shaoxing wine, sticky rice, sambal oelek, palm sugar, mirin, wasabi paste, and filé powder.

D'Artagnan
280 Wilson Avenue
Newark, NJ 07105
800-327-8246 or 973-344-0565
www.dartagnan.com
Duck breasts, frozen beef marrow, truffle paste, and other fine meat products shipped overnight or priority.

Dean & DeLuca
Catalog Center
2526 East 36th Street,
North Circle
Wichita, KS 67219
800-221-7714
www.deanddeluca.com
A variety of specialty foods, including fennel pollen, white truffle paste, and caviar.

Earthy Delights
1161 East Clark Road, Ste. 260
DeWitt, MI 48820
800-367-4709
www.earthy.com
A variety of specialty foods and produce, including ramps, in season.

Japanese Green Tea Online
6-81-203 Koyoen, Hinode-cho
Nishinomiya-shi, Japan
866-448-4412
www.japanesegreenteaonline.com
Matcha and other Japanese teas and tea accessories.

Kalustyan's
Marhaba International, Inc.
123 Lexington Avenue
New York, NY 10016
800-352-3451
www.kalustyans.com
A wide variety of spices and specialty foods, including bonito flakes, dried whole chilies, sambal oelek, fresh curry leaves, pomegranate molasses, tamarind concentrate and paste, rice wine vinegar, mirin, jaggery, palm sugar, quinoa, and wasabi powder.

Kam Man Food Products
Customer Support Department
200 Canal Street
New York, NY 10013
Tel: 212-571-0330/0331
Fax: 212-966-7085
Szechwan peppercorns, tamarind paste, five-spice powder, fish sauce, bamboo skewers, and bean curd sheets.

Pacific Rim Gourmet
4905 Morena Boulevard, Ste. 1313
San Diego, CA 92117
800-910-9657
www.pacificrim-gourmet.com
Kitchenware and ingredients, including steamers, sushi mats, tapioca shreds and pearls, coconut milk, and a variety of spices and sauces.

Penzeys Spices
P.O. Box 924
Brookfield, WI 53008
800-741-7787
www.penzeys.com
Dried herbs and spices, including coriander, cardamom pods and seeds, filé powder, and brown mustard seeds.

The Stash Tea Company
P. O. Box 910
Portland, OR 97207
800-826-4218
www.stashtea.com
Matcha and other specialty teas and tea accessories.

Sur La Table
Catalog Division
P.O. Box 34707
Seattle, WA 98124
800-243-0852
www.surlatable.com
A selection of basic cooking tools and equipment, as well as an assortment of hard-to-find specialty items for cooking and baking.

Temple of Thai
P.O. Box 112
Carroll, IA 51401
877-811-8773
www.templeofthai.com
Thai cooking ingredients and utensils, including canned coconut milk, sticky rice, rice noodles, sambal oelek, fish sauce, dried whole red chilies, fresh Thai chilies, fresh lemon-grass, and tamarind paste.

Urbani Truffles USA
380 Meadowbrook Road
North Wales, PA 19454
215-699-8780
www.urbanitruffles.com
White Alba truffles, white truffle purée, caviar, black truffles, truffle oil, mushrooms, smoked fish.

Williams-Sonoma
3250 Van Ness Avenue
San Francisco, CA 94109
800-541-2233
www.williams-sonoma.com
A wide variety of cooking supplies; also carries demi-glace and other specialty foods.

Zingerman's Delicatessen
422 Detroit Street
Ann Arbor, MI 48104
888-636-8162
www.zingermans.com
Fennel pollen, coarse salt, olive oil, balsamic vinegar, cheeses, baked goods.

Conversion Charts

Weight Measurements

Standard U.S.	Ounces	Metric
1 ounce	1	30 g
¼ pound	4	125 g
½ pound	8	250 g
1 pound	16	500 g
1½ pounds	24	750 g
2 pounds	32	1 kg
2½ pounds	40	1.25 kg
3 pounds	48	1.5 kg

Volume Measurements

Standard U.S.	Fluid Ounces	Metric
1 tablespoon	½	15 ml
2 tablespoons	1	30 ml
3 tablespoons	1½	45 ml
¼ cup (4 tablespoons)	2	60 ml
6 tablespoons	3	90 ml
½ cup (8 tablespoons)	4	125 ml
1 cup	8	250 ml
1 pint (2 cups)	16	500 ml
4 cups	32	1 l

Oven Temperatures

Fahrenheit	Celsius	Gas Mark
250°	120°	½
275°	135°	1
300°	150°	2
325°	165°	3
350°	180°	4
375°	190°	5
400°	200°	6
425°	220°	7

NOTE: For ease of use, measurements have been rounded off.

Conversion Factors

OUNCES TO GRAMS: Multiply the ounce figure by 28.3 to get the number of grams.

POUNDS TO GRAMS: Multiply the pound figure by 453.59 to get the number of grams.

POUNDS TO KILOGRAMS: Multiply the pound figure by 0.45 to get the number of kilograms.

OUNCES TO MILLILITERS: Multiply the ounce figure by 30 to get the number of milliliters.

CUPS TO LITERS: Multiply the cup figure by 0.24 to get the number of liters.

FAHRENHEIT TO CELSIUS: Subtract 32 from the Fahrenheit figure, multiply by 5, then divide by 9 to get the Celsius figure.

Contributors

AVALON
270 Adelaide Street West
Toronto, Ontario
M5H 1X6 Canada
Phone: (416) 979-9918
Fax: (416) 599-2006
www.avalonrestaurant.ca

BACCHANALIA
1198 Howell Mill Road,
Ste. 100
Atlanta, GA 30318
Phone: (404) 365-0410
Fax: (404) 365-8020
www.starprovisions.com

**THE RESTAURANT AT
HOTEL BEL-AIR**
701 Stone Canyon Road
Los Angeles, CA 90077
Phone: (310) 472-1211
Fax: (310) 909-1630
www.hotelbelair.com

BLUE GINGER
583 Washington Street
Wellesley, MA 02482
Phone: (781) 283-5790
Fax: (781) 283-5772
www.ming.com

CAFÉ BOULUD
20 East 76th Street
New York, NY 10021
Phone: (212) 772-2600
www.danielnyc.com

CASANOVA
5th Avenue between Mission
and San Carlos
Carmel, CA 93921
Phone: (831) 625-0501
Fax: (831) 625-9799
www.casanovarestaurant.com

CASTLE HILL INN AND RESORT
590 Ocean Drive
Newport, RI 02840
Phone: (401) 849-3800
Fax: (401) 849-3838
www.castlehillinn.com

COMMANDER'S PALACE
1403 Washington Avenue
New Orleans, LA 70130
Phone: (504) 899-8221
Fax: (504) 891-3242
www.commanderspalace.com

40 SARDINES
11942 Roe Avenue
Overland Park, KS 66209
Phone: (913) 451-1040
Fax: (913) 451-1048
www.40sardines.com

**THE GRILL AT
THE DRISKILL HOTEL**
604 Brazos Street
Austin, TX 78701
Phone: (512) 391-7162
Fax: (512) 391-7222
www.driskillgrill.com

**THE BISTRO AT
HOTEL MAISON DE VILLE**
727 Rue Toulouse
New Orleans, LA 70130
Phone: (504) 528-9206
Fax: (504) 528-9939
www.hotelmaisondeville.com

MARCEL'S
2401 Pennsylvania Avenue NW
Washington, D.C 20037
Phone: (202) 296-1166
Fax: (202) 296-6466
www,marcelsdc.com

MOOSE'S
1652 Stockton Street
San Francisco, CA 94133
Phone: (415) 989-7800
Fax: (415) 989-7838
www.mooses.com

NORTH POND
2610 North Cannon Drive
Chicago, IL 60614
Phone: (773) 477-5845
www.northpondrestaurant.com

TABLA
11 Madison Avenue
New York, NY 10010
Phone: (212) 889-0667
Fax: (212) 889-3865

VETRI
1312 Spruce Street
Philadelphia, PA 19107
Phone: (215) 732-3478
Fax: (215) 732-3487
www.vetrirestaurant.com

WILD GINGER
1401 3rd Avenue
Seattle, WA 98101-2105
Phone: (206) 623-4450
Fax: (206) 623-8265

YOSHI'S
510 Embarcadero West
Oakland, CA 94607
Phone: (510) 238-9200
Fax: (510) 238-4551
www.yoshis.com

CREDITS

pp 4–5 Henri Matisse. *The Knife Thrower* © 2004 Succession H. Matisse, Paris/Artists Rights Society (ARS), New York

p 8 Henri Matisse. *Horse, Rider and Clown* © 2004 Succession H. Matisse, Paris/Artists Rights Society (ARS), New York

pp 12–13 Henri Matisse. *The Codomas* © 2004 Succession H. Matisse, Paris/Artists Rights Society (ARS), New York

p 18 Henri Matisse. *The Sword Swallower* © 2004 Succession H. Matisse, Paris/Artists Rights Society (ARS), New York

pp 20–21 Henri Matisse. *The Heart* © 2004 Succession H. Matisse, Paris/Artists Rights Society (ARS), New York

p 25 Henri Matisse. *Icarus* © 2004 Succession H. Matisse, Paris/Artists Rights Society (ARS), New York

pp 26–27 Henri Matisse. *Destiny* © 2004 Succession H. Matisse, Paris/Artists Rights Society (ARS), New York

p 28 Henri Matisse. *Lagoon* © 2004 Succession H. Matisse, Paris/Artists Rights Society (ARS), New York

pp 28–29 "A Warm Summer in San Francisco," by Carolyn Miller, was first published in *Nimrod International Journal*, and was republished in *Constant Lover* (Protean Press, 2001).

p 30 Moonrise at Union Station in Toronto, Canada Grant Faint/Getty Images

p 40 photo by Jeff Kemph

p 48 Car Lights, Downtown Los Angeles, CA, USA Steve Lewis/Getty Images

p 58 Huge snow-covered tree in Boston Common, the oldest public park in the United States. Medford Taylor/ NATIONAL GEOGRAPHIC IMAGE COLLECTION/Getty Images

p 68 © Molly Stevens (www.portraitsatparties.com)

p 78 Trees Growing on Rocky Headland in Carmel © Douglas Peebles/Corbis

p 96 Bourbon Street © Jose Fuste Raga/Corbis

p 106 Plaza Time Tower in Country Club Plaza © Richard Cummins/Corbis

p 116 University of Texas Tower Jonathan Gregson/Getty Images

p 124 Jazz Musician Playing Under Street Light © Bob Krist/Corbis

p 132 Washington Monument © Craig Aurness/Corbis

p 142 © Kirk Crippens (www.crippensphoto.com)

p 150 Skyscrapers Along the Chicago River © Richard Cummins/Corbis

p 160 42nd Street and the Chrysler Building in New York City at Twilight Mitchell Funk/Getty Images

p 170 Independence Day Fireworks at Philadelphia Museum of Art © Bob Krist/Corbis

p 178 Sailboat Race © Morton Beebe/Corbis

p 186 © Kirk Crippens (www.crippensphoto.com)

ACKNOWLEDGMENTS

I would like to thank the many people who made this volume possible. My deepest gratitude to the chefs and proprietors of the restaurants who generously contributed their recipes to the cookbook: Chris McDonald of Avalon; Anne Quatrano and Clifford Harrison of Bacchanalia; Carlos Lopes, Roland Venturini, and Douglas Dodd of Hotel Bel-Air; Ming Tsai and Sarah Hearn of Blue Ginger; Daniel Boulud and Georgette Farkas of Café Boulud; Walter and Gaston Georis, Didier Dutertre, and Leah Chism of Casanova; Natalie Ward and Casey Riley of Castle Hill Inn and Resort; Ella Brennan, Tory McPhail, and Sally Graves of Commander's Palace; Debbie Gold and Michael Smith of 40 Sardines; Jeffrey Trigger and David Bull of The Driskill Hotel and The Grill at The Driskill; Dmitri Veltsos and Greg Picolo of Hotel Maison de Ville and The Bistro at Hotel Maison de Ville; Robert and Polly Wiedmaier of Marcel's, Ed and Mary Etta Moose and Jeffrey Amber of Moose's, Bruce Sherman of North Pond; Danny Meyer and Floyd Cardoz of Tabla; Marc Vetri of Vetri Restaurant; Rick and Ann Yoder of Wild Ginger; Yoshi Akiba of Yoshi's.

I am forever grateful to Kenny Barron, Bob Sheppard, Dave Ellis, Peter Barshay, and Lewis Nash for making this recording a dream come true. Special thanks to Peter Barshay for the arrangements. Thanks also to recording and mixing engineer Dave Luke, assistant engineer James Willetts, and George Horn of Fantasy Studios, Berkeley, for the mastering.

Sincere thanks once again to Paul Moore for his stunning food photography; to Amy Nathan for her extraordinary food styling; and to Sara Slavin for her stylish tableware and props.

Deepest gratitude to my longtime editor, Carolyn Miller, for her beautiful poem, expert advice, and editorial guidance. Acknowledgment and fond regards to Bill Minor and Taj Mahal. Thanks once again to Jenny Barry of Jennifer Barry Design for her book and cover design, and thanks also to Kristen Wurz of Jennifer Barry Design.

I want to thank Sarah Creider for her invaluable assistance during this entire project. Thanks to Kirk Crippens for his photography of the music instruments and to Alexandra Ivanoff of 1168 Studios, San Francisco for the use of the Steinway grand piano. Grateful acknowledgments to Sharlene Swacke, for her unfailing grace, dignity, and beauty under pressure; to Tim Forney, for his heart and humor; to Lisa Parker, Ned Waring, and Dave Cados, for their energy and attention to detail; and to Erick Villatoro and Isidro Montesinos, for their excellent work.

And, as always, I am especially grateful to my daughters Claire and Caitlin, and to my husband John, for their adventurous appetites and their love.

INDEX